MASTER THE MODS!

MINECRAFT® SECRETS

& Cool Ways to Take Your Building Games to Another Level

MASTER THE MODS!

This book is available in quantity at special discounts for your group or organization. For further information, contact:

Triumph Books LLC
814 North Franklin Street
Chicago, Illinois 60610
Phone: (312) 337-0747
www.triumphbooks.com

Printed in U.S.A.
ISBN: 978-1-62937-184-9

Content packaged by Mojo Media, Inc.
Joe Funk: Editor
Jason Hinman: Creative Director
Trevor Talley: Writer

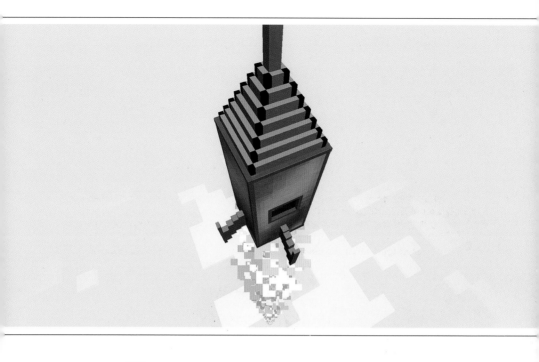

Contents

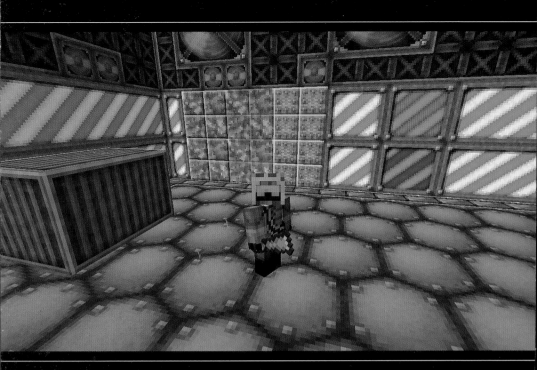

Introduction

It's always said that what you can do in Minecraft is limited only by your imagination. This is true, but only to a point. While you certainly can build just about anything you can think of in the regular game, which is often called "vanilla" Minecraft, the palette of blocks and items that you can use to build your creations is limited to what comes with the game. Sure you can combine them together to make them look similar to almost anything, but what if you had more to use, more to choose from? What could you create then, if you truly had no limits?

That is the question this book answers.

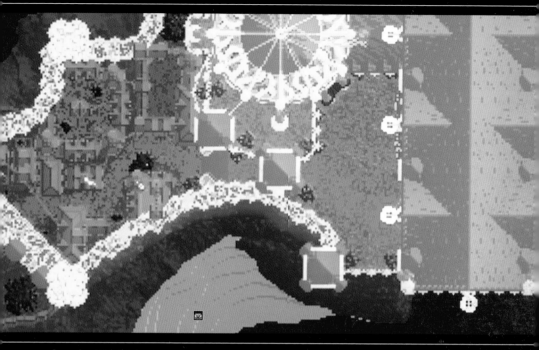

Opposite: With this book, you'll soon be like player Drullkus here, decked out in all sorts of fancy new gear surrounded by a heap of new, awesome blocks. Above: See the world of Minecraft like never before, sometimes quite literally like with this minimap mod called VoxelMap.

THE WORLD OF MODS

That we even can answer that question is because of one of the best, not-all-that-secret secrets in gaming: There is another facet of Minecraft outside of the vanilla game that adds these extra items and truly does turn the game into whatever the human mind can come up with, and it is accessible to any player. Millions of Minecrafters are already taking advantage of this fascinating, thrilling semi-secret world within Minecraft, and in fact, if you've ever been on a Minecraft server and wondered how the heck they got all those crazy new blocks or how they do things like let you play paintball in Minecraft, you were actually taking part in it without even knowing it.

We're talking about the world of Minecraft "mods," a term that is short for modifications and which refers to code created by fans and inserted into the regular game. Mods are designed to add amazing new features to change Minecraft in an incredibly wide variety of ways, each of which came entirely from the imagination of players just like you and all of which are super cool in the unique ways that they change the game.

Mods can let you do everything from build a rocketship and fly to the moon, to going deep into ancient pyramids to battle mighty Egyptian queens with your magic Bow in mods like Atum.

WHAT CAN MODS DO?

These changes can be just about anything, from new items and blocks to new mobs to fight to whole new, fully-realized ways to play the game. Want to have a realistic gunfight in a fully-decked out Wild West world in Minecraft? Want to fly a plane around a roaring tornado that's ripping up a mighty mountain range, in Minecraft? Want to battle forty-block-tall monsters by casting blistering and crackling magic spells from the walls of a fantasy-land castle, populated with its own denizens? Want to turn into a hamster and fly to space in a rocket?

You can do all of that and more with mods.

Some mods will even change the way the very land generates (ExtraBiomesXL and Biomes O' Plenty) or let you take pictures of your world in brand new, cool-looking ways (Optifine and Mineshot).

The options are truly endless. There are just so very many mods out there, from the small and subtle to those that absolutely change the game from the ground up, making it barely resemble its original self. There are mods that simply change a bit of the look of Minecraft, maybe adding a new indicator to the Heads Up Display, or making it a bit prettier. There are mods that do very specific things, like adding in a series of new mobs of a certain kind (like fantasy monsters, or real-world animals) or a set of things to use for cooking. There are mods that are all about adding new systems to the 'Craft, some of which are quite simple and some of which make Redstone look like child's play. And then there are huge mods meant to essentially build a whole new game within Minecraft, giving the player almost endless things to do and changing the look and feel so much that it can make it feel like the first time you picked up the game all over again. Basically, if you can think it, there's probably a mod of it, and there are so many to explore that you could spend a lifetime doing so.

Moments like this, where a dragon named The King battles a huge lizard called Mobzilla, can only happen in mods (in this case the excellent Orespawn mod).

WHY IT'S A GREAT TIME TO GET INTO MODS

As it is for many popular games, the modding community has been a major part of Minecraft since its early days, but right now it is perhaps the strongest its ever been, and it's certainly one of the best and most comprehensive modding communities in the history of games. Thousands of highly talented, creative people all over the world pour countless hours of hard work into creating, updating and maintaining mods for Minecraft each year, and the mods they've created have gotten incredibly good. And, as is entirely appropriate considering the staggering quality of some of these mods, a huge community within the larger Minecraft community has grown up around these mods with countless players loading them up and creating undoubtedly some of the best things ever made in the game.

Because of the massive amount of mods out there, the incredible communities that have grown up around them, Minecraft's continued popularity, and great new updates, there has never been a better time to get into modding. This book is designed to help you do just that, by showing you a bit on what mods are, how to get them working in your own games, and then taking you on a tour of what mods are out there right now, waiting for you.

WHAT YOU CAN EXPECT FROM THIS BOOK

This is not a comprehensive book of everything to know about mods, or a directory of all the mods out there; a book like that would be thousands of pages long and would have to be updated every other day. That's how many mods there are and how fast they change.

What it is, is an introduction to mods for the new folks, and a celebration of the state of mods right now in 2015 for the rest of us. What we've gathered here is meant to represent not all of the best mods in the world, and indeed we've had to leave a few excellent ones off for space reasons, but instead is meant to show you a curated collection of mods that represent the many different facets of the modding world. That's why you'll see plenty of the big-name mods like Thaumcraft or FTB Infinity, which have big teams of people working on them all the time, but you'll also see smaller mods here like Fex's Random Stuff Mod or Xaero's Minimap, each of which is solely created and maintained by a single passionate player.

Whether you are one of those who has been into modding since the get-go, or this is your first time hearing about them, this book will give you information on over 100 mods, many of which the veterans might not have even heard of, and all of which are thoroughly awesome. Frankly, if you love Minecraft, we think there's not much chance that you'll be able to get to the end of this book without wanting to drop it and install at least one of these right away, and that's exactly the goal we're setting out to achieve.

There really is no limit to what can happen with mods, and we think the fun that is out there waiting to be had with them is equally limitless. So let's stop just talking about how cool mods are, and actually get into a few! Strap yourself in readers, because you're about to start a wild journey through the crazy, Crafty world of Minecraft mods, and it may very well shake up your entire concept of how to play the world's favorite video game.

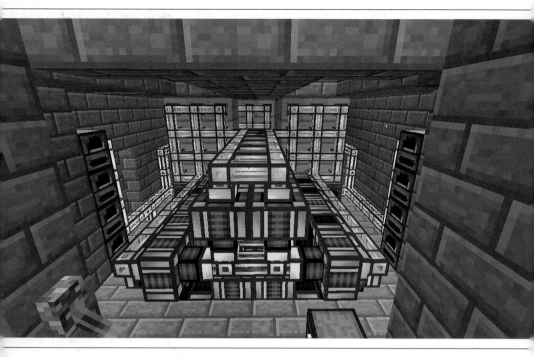

The Many Kinds Of **Mods**

When someone makes a mod, they're actually going in and writing computer code to make changes to the game, which then needs to be loaded into the game's regular code. Because of this, mods can vary greatly in all respects, from how many changes they make and how big those changes are, to how big the files in the mod are and how they get loaded into the game's normal code.

It's useful when getting an idea of how mods work, what they can do for your game, and just generally what mods are out there to separate them into different categories. We've done this in three different ways to help introduce you to the world of mods, first by breaking them into sizes, giving each mod a complexity rating, and also by separating into categories by what they add. There are almost as many types of mods as there are mods themselves (of which there are thousands), and the lines can blur for some between the categories (like Thaumcraft, which adds items but does enough with systems to be included in that category) but most of them fit under one or more of these definitions:

Opposite: There are tech mods that make Minecraft a world of extreme automation (image by Drullkus)... Above: ...and then there are mods that are all about plain fun and adding in cool things from other universes, like the Pixelmon mod seen here.

MODS OF DIFFERENT SIZES

Size is an important factor when it comes to mods, because a mod's size typically determines two things that players need to know: how difficult the mod will be to install, and how much it will change the vanilla game. How much it changes the game is something that matters quite a lot. Sometimes players are looking to change the entirety of their game, while others just want a little tweak. This is even more important when trying to mix various mods together in one game, something we'll talk about more in the next chapter.

BubbaDogface, the writer of this book's trusty Minecraft pup, owes his name and ability to be a Creeper hunter to a small mod called Doggy Talents. Isn't he a cute little dogface?

The sizes of mods:

Tiny mods: Tiny mods are ones that make minimal, barely noticeable additions or changes to the game. Utility mods are often tiny mods, adding just a little change to the Heads Up Display, as are mods like our Odd Mod Spotlight mod Second Screen, which adds a very lightweight system that lets you chat and see data on your Minecraft server from another device. One very notable and desirable feature of tiny mods is that they are often so lightweight that they are very easy to run at the same time as other mods. In fact, they're so easy to install with other mods that tiny mods are often put in modpacks with many other, often much bigger mods.

Small mods: Smaller mods usually tweak or add just one small thing or segment of the game. For instance Fex's Random Stuff Mod just adds a bunch of items. Playing with small mods usually doesn't feel all that different from the regular game, there's just a little more to do or a few more entities to interact with. Small mods often work together very well as well, similar to tiny mods, if not quite so easily.

Mid-sized mods: These are mods that make either one significant change or a few smaller changes together. An example of this would be the ICBM Mod, which really isn't a very large mod, but it does add items, a new set of crafting recipes and a new way to do combat. Mythical Creatures is another mid-sized mod, really just adding mobs and a few items, but adding a ton of mobs that are very different from the regular ones and which can make a big difference to the game.

Big mods: As opposed to small mods, you'll notice when you load up a game with a big mod. They tend to change large parts of the game significantly, making it a mostly or entirely new experience. As an example, one such mod is the Tinkers' Construct, which takes the regular method of crafting tools and items through a Crafting Table and makes it much more complicated, adding multiple types of crafting stations, tables and forges and making players use Patterns and build each individual part of the tool they want. Another example is the Aether mod, which adds an entire new dimension in the sky. These mods are ones which can't be ignored in a game.

Full conversion mods: Full conversion mods are big mods that are the most noticeable, because they change the game in huge ways, usually so much so that the objective when playing them is something new. This category includes mods like The Crafting Dead, which aims to turn the Minecraft world into a zombie apocalypse wasteland. It includes guns, advanced zombies and new systems for thirst, whether you can be seen or heard, temperature, and even whether you're bleeding. Even cooler, it also adds in new specially generated maps that simulate the world of a zombie apocalypse. Though you can (and should) build in The Crafting Dead, the goal is much more about surviving zombie attacks and living in a much harsher world than it is about mining and the like, making it a full conversion of the game.

Modpacks: The biggest of all, modpacks are groups of mods that have been put together by players and/or mod creators in curated packages so that they all load together. These are the best place to start out when it comes to mods, as they are usually very easy to load, and they give you the chance to experience many of the best mods right away. Additionally, mods can be very picky about working together normally, but modpacks are specially put together so that they just work without you having to do much of anything. That being said, stacking mods very quickly changes the game heavily, and some of the modpacks can get a bit intimidating with all of their many, many new things (for instance, FTB Infinity with over 100 mods).

Here you see two types of mods mixed together, a biomes mod, and a few different visual mods including shaders, a program that tweaks the visuals of Minecraft (Optifine) and an image taking mod.

MODS OF DIFFERENT TYPES

We've organized our book based on a way of looking at mods, which divides them by type. We did this because knowing a mod's type is what tells you the most about a mod, and by "type," we're referring to the primary thing that each mod actually does.

It should be noted that many mods actually do a few things, and some of those things might fit in another category other than the one the mod is listed in with this book. The line between mods is often quite fluid, and it's easy to put many of these mods in multiple categories. Quite a few mods out there do quite a lot, but we've categorized mods as we have based on the main thing that they are known for and do.

With that in mind, here are the primary categories for each type of mod:

Utility mods: These are mods meant to be useful to the player in some specific way, making gameplay just a little easier or more informative, and they're usually very small. Utility mods do things like add a better map to your interface, tell you the exact amount of daylight/night left, or make it easier to find friends. They also tend to work with other mods easily, as they're often among the tiniest mods that are out there.

The Many Kinds Of Mods

Item mods: Item mods are those whose primary purpose is to do just what the title says and add a whole bunch of items. Some items mods also add in some systems, like Still Hungry's new cooking system on the Stove, but these are usually very simple and not the primary objective of the mod. Items mods are pretty popular among the categories because they don't require a lot of learning of new things and are very controllable by the player. Think of it as adding more toppings to a pizza: there's just more to experience, and the overall flavor is just that much more complex and exciting, but it's still pizza at its core.

Land and biome design mods: The world around you in Minecraft is already pretty complex with its many biomes, but it can always get more interesting! These mods are those whose point is to make the land more complex or otherwise change it. Some add new biomes or dimensions, like Twilight Forest or ExtraBiomesXL, while others do littler tweaks like Mineralogy's new way of distributing rock.

Combat mods: More items to fight with, ways to fight better, and new ways to fight! Some people don't care much about combat in Minecraft, choosing to build, because the basic system really isn't very extensive. It shouldn't come as much of a surprise to anyone that some people have really wanted better combat in Minecraft, and that's exactly what combat mods provide. Some do this heavily, like Mine and Blade's new system of weapon holding and items, and some just add a little to basic combat, like BetterPvP.

Mob mods: Who doesn't want more cuddly (or not so cuddly) creatures to play with in their Minecraft world? Mob mods are actually surprisingly few, perhaps because it can get pretty crowded pretty quick if you overdo it on creatures (which is also hard on your computer), but the ones that do this well give Minecraft a fuller feel, making the world feel like a place where things are constantly happening, and there's a potential friend or foe around every tree.

Building mods: Many mods add blocks; in fact a majority of them do. Because it's so common, and so many mods that do so belong more in another category, that's not what we mean when we talk about building mods. Instead, these are mods that do the building for you, making it much quicker to create structures. This isn't a highly common type of mod, but they are out there.

Adventure enhancers: We use this term to refer to those mods which all have in common the fact that make "fantasy and adventure" part of Minecraft more detailed and complex. That's not really a technical term of course, and this is a pretty wide category of mods, but we think it makes sense to group these mods together. That's partly because the sense of going on an adventure in a fantastical land is such a big part of Minecraft's charm, so it makes sense to focus on these mods as a category, and they also just work very well together. Some of our favorite mods fall into this category, as do many of the most downloaded mods on the internet.

Even a few minutes inside vanilla Minecraft would give you the knowledge that the tech you're seeing in this image by Drullkus just could never happen in regular Minecraft.

Magic, tech, and crafting systems: Another of the most popular mod types, these mods add new systems of doing things, giving players something to learn beyond basic crafting and Redstone. Sometimes this is just one small system, like the Railcraft or ICBM mods, but sometimes it adds so much and/or is so dang complex that it makes figuring out Redstone wiring seem like child's play, like Thermal Expansion or Applied Energistics. Engineering-types, those that like the idea of super-fancy bases with a lot of automation, figuring stuff out, and learning a new way of thinking are often the kind of people that end up loving the mods in this category.

Visual mods: We do love Minecraft's iconic, pared-down, pixely look, but mods give people the chance to change up the way the computer represents a Minecraft world onscreen and do it their way. Sometimes the vision of Minecraft's visual mod creators is a massive change to make the vanilla world look beautiful, such as the way Shaders reconfigure and heavily enhance the lighting system in Minecraft, and sometimes it's as simple as adding a way to take awesome screenshots.

Modloader packs: Modloaders are programs that you can use to launch big modpacks, which are collections of many mods. These loaders make the modpacks load smoothly without much input from the user (at least, that's the idea), which greatly cuts down on the work you

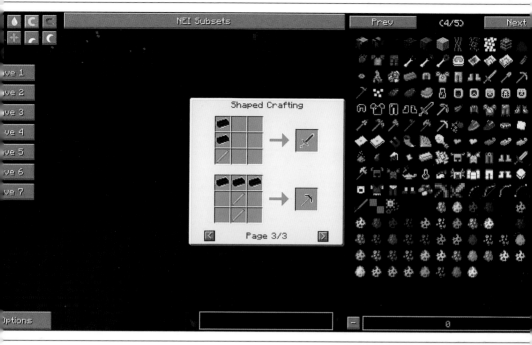

Just look at all the new menus, systems and items that just a couple of mods can add to Minecraft!

have to do to mix mods. We've separated some mods from the biggest modloaders out there because many of the world's most popular modpacks are held under the umbrella of the two big modloaders, the Feed the Beast loader and the Technic loader, often exclusively. This is great for us players, as it means that the experts working for these loaders keep track of everything for us, making sure all mods work, are up to date and work well together. Loaders are both a great place for new mod players to start out, as they make it easy to get them going, and for mod veterans, as many of the best and most complex mods are in this category.

MODS OF DIFFERENT COMPLEXITY

As we've mentioned, not all mods are equal. Some do a lot but are pretty simple, others are small but complex, and there's everything in-between. Because of this, we've added a little scale to this book that quickly tells you how complex a mod is. This is more of a general guideline to give you info on what to expect, and not a hard-and-fast technical rating, as people will often vary on what they think is complex from person to person. The idea is to let you know at a glance whether adding a mod will take a lot of learning, or whether it will be a quick and easy addition.

To this end, we've rated each mod from 0 to 5 Diamonds, with 0 being the least complicated, and 5 being the most complicated mods or modpacks that there are.

Screenshot: Minecraft® ™ & © 2009–2015 Mojang/Notch

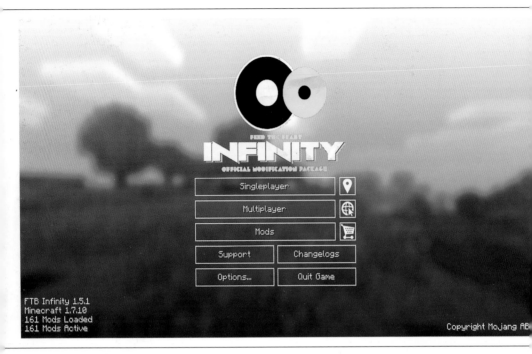

How To Install Your **Mods**

Right, so here's the one tricky bit when it comes to mods: Installing mods can be a bit of a pain.

Mods are just plain fun, once you get them installed, that is. We think that the experiences in modded Minecraft are as good as any others in gaming, bar none, and a lot of people out there agree with us.

That being said, getting a mod installed can (but won't always) take a bit of work.

Typically it's not hard at all. Most Minecraft mods are loaded the same way, and you just have to learn it once to get it forever. Those kinds of mods go through the Forge program, where you only have to worry about making sure all mods are for the same version of Minecraft and that you put the mod into the correct folder.

Opposite: If you've done your work right, you should be seeing custom modded versions of Minecraft just like this one in no time flat! Above: It's only a matter of time before you start seeing Minecraft's world in a whole new way.

Sometimes, though, it takes a little doing. Each computer is different, and each situation is unique when getting a mod working, both for the computer and for the mod. This book and this chapter can guide you to a point, but it's so different from one mod to the next that you always want to read the mod's instructions on its page and follow them to the letter. Luckily almost all mod creators include detailed instructions at the mod's link, and we've included the links to every mod in this book, so you should be able to easily find each mod's specific installation instructions.

Sometimes even that isn't enough, though, and there's always the chance that you might have to ask for help in the Minecraft Forums or on the mod's page. Don't hesitate to do that, though remember to remain polite. This is also part of the mod culture; mods are made by fans, so they're rarely an exact science, and getting mods to run is a traditional part of the experience for all games, and all gamers seeking to mod them. Each mod has an online presence somewhere, and if you have the time to invest in it, you will be able to get almost every mod running on your own rig.

You'll become very familiar with pages like this one when you start getting into modding.

The hope is that you'll be able to avoid doing too much work for a mod, though. A little instruction in basic mod installation will be all you need 80% of the time, and that's what we've got for you here.

WHERE TO GET MODS

We've included a link to every mod in this book (except for the ones that go through a modloader, which don't require a link), but in general when looking for a mod, there are four locations at which you'll find most mods:

Planet Minecraft: The prime directory of all Minecraft creations, including maps, texture packs and, as is most pertinent to this book, mods. The vast majority of mods have a Planet Minecraft page that has a link to download them, info about the mod, photos, and/or video of the mod and a comment section. Not all PMC profiles are kept totally up-to-date, however, though many are.

The Minecraft Forums are an indispensible resource for anyone interested in mods, as you can not only get mods there, you can also learn how to install them and speak to the creators and community, which is especially great if you're having any trouble getting a mod to run.

The Minecraft Forum: The Minecraft Forum is the other primary website where mods keep a major presence, along with Planet Minecraft. Though they are a bit less formal of a project-holding site, in that the entries for the mods are just forum posts (though often well-structured and heavily informed ones). At the current time it is more common for a mod to have an up-to-date, well-crafted Minecraft Forum post than a good Planet Minecraft post. Often, though, the big mods have both. In this book you'll find more Minecraft Forum links than any other, and you won't go wrong from following one, when it comes to getting mods working.

The Curse Page: The Curse company is extensively involved in online gaming, and they have a major presence within the Minecraft community. Not only does the Minecraft Wiki, the prime repository for Minecraft knowledge online, fall under the Curse banner, Curse also hosts downloads for many Minecraft mods. A lot of the big mods have a Curse page in addition to a PMC and/or Minecraft Forum page. Though these don't have the comment section interaction or the pure Minecraft focus that the other mod links have, Curse pages are very reliable and consistently updated, and some mod creators consider their Curse page to be the best one to share with potential users.

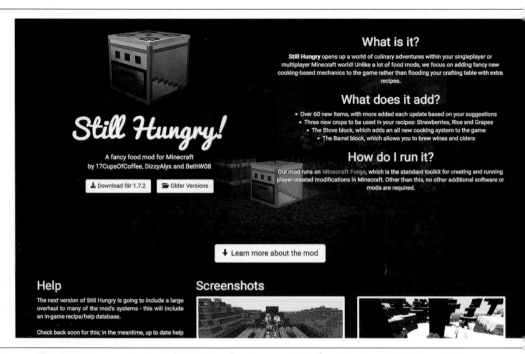

What is it?

Still Hungry opens up a world of culinary adventures within your singleplayer or multiplayer Minecraft world! Unlike a lot of food mods, we focus on adding fancy new cooking-based mechanics to the game rather than flooding your crafting table with extra recipes.

What does it add?

- Over 60 new items, with more added each update based on your suggestions
- Three new crops to be used in your recipes: Strawberries, Rice and Grapes
- The Stove block, which adds an all new cooking system to the game
- The Barrel block, which allows you to brew wines and ciders

How do I run it?

Our mod runs on Minecraft Forge, which is the standard toolkit for creating and running player-created modifications in Minecraft. Other than this, no other additional software or mods are required.

Still Hungry!

A fancy food mod for Minecraft
by 17CupsOfCoffee, DizzyAlyx and BethW08

⬇ Download for 1.7.2   🗀 Older Versions

⬇ Learn more about the mod

Help

The next version of Still Hungry is going to include a large overhaul to many of the mod's systems - this will include an in-game recipe/help database.

Check back soon for this; in the meantime, up to date help

Screenshots

This is an example of an individual mod creator page for the lovely food mod Still Hungry! Using these pages is one great way to help mod creators out a bit.

Individual Mod Creator Pages: Mod creators don't make a lot of money doing what they do. They work on a game that already makes its money separately, and the only way they get compensated is from user donations or from getting hits on their mod links. By far the best way to support mod creators is to use their own website to download a mod, as it will directly reflect on hits on their site and will direct you to the download link that pays them the most , both of which earn them money. Not only that, but creators' websites always have the up-to-the-minute download info, updates and guides to mods, so they are always preferable when it comes to getting a new mod.

The rule is this: Google it, and try to find the personal page for the mod creator. If you can't, go with PMC, the Minecraft Forum, or Curse. Avoid most other sites at all costs, as few good mods have no presence at the main sites, and there are definitely sites out there with some dubious downloads on offer.

The links you need for forge are down at the bottom of this page. There are a few different ones, but the Install link typically is the best one.

FORGE: THE PROGRAM THAT MAKES MOST MODS WORK

http://files.minecraftforge.net/

The first step to getting Minecraft mods going on your computer is to install the Forge mod loading program.

To do this, you'll have to download the Forge installer from the link above and then run it. At the link above, simply scroll down to the "Downloads" section, and then pick the version of Minecraft you would like to run mods in. Note: this is most likely going to be Minecraft 1.8, 1.7.10, or 1.6.4. If you decide you want to run mods for a different version of Minecraft later, you'll just come back to this link and download and install that one.

To actually download the file, make sure you've clicked on the version you want, and then look below where it says "Download Recommended" (if it only says "Download Latest," look there instead). Click the "Installer" button (Windows users can also just use the Installer-win" button, but either will work), and then save the file to your computer.

Screenshot: Minecraft® ™ & © 2009–2015 Mojang/Notch

Mod system installer

Welcome to the simple Forge installer.
Forge 11.14.1.1402

Data kindly mirrored by Creeper Host

◉ **Install client**

◯ **Install server**

◯ **Extract**

/Users/foldersohard/Library/Application Support/minecr   ...

          Cancel   OK

Forge really is quite simple to install, especially since it tells you if you did it right at the end!

Before you open that file and install it, you need to make sure that you have opened Minecraft at least once. Most likely you already have, but if you're jumping right into modding, make sure you open the game first and then close out again. This must be done because certain files and folders Forge needs aren't created until Minecraft runs for the first time.

When that's done, run the file you downloaded from Forge. It will pop up a window asking if you want to "Install Client," "Install Server," or "Extract." Select "Install Client," and ignore the file location at the bottom and just hit OK. It should then show that it's downloading and installing Forge, and if you did it right, you'll see it tell you that it was successful.

On a Mac, this is the menu you want to drop down while pressing the "alt" key in order to find the Library. On a PC, use the Run program and type in "%AppData%/.minecraft" to find the Minecraft folder.

FINDING AND INSTALLING MODS FOR FORGE
To actually get mods loaded into Forge, you will need to do a few things.

1. Get some mods! This is the easy part- just go to one of the links in this book, or head to Planet Minecraft, the Minecraft Forums, or the Curse webpage and search around for mods. There are tons on each of these, and a good idea for which to pick is to go with those that have a lot of downloads (each site lists these differently, though for the Forums you'll just have to look at how many comments the mod's page has instead of download numbers). Make sure that you are getting the correct mod for the version of Forge you have installed (and remember that you can always download and install other versions of Forge).

Note: When installing mods for the first time, you should always add just one mod at a time. This way if a mod causes Minecraft to crash, you know which one did it. In fact, we highly recommend that you only install one mod period for your first go at modded Minecraft, and wait until you get the hang of how to install mods before adding any more to a single game.

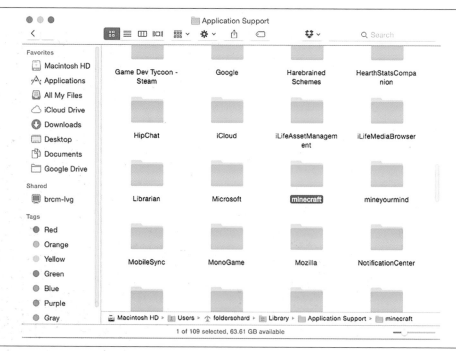

There's that pesky Minecraft folder! You'll be coming back to this a lot if you get into modding, so remember how to find it quickly to save time.

2. Find the mods folder. To run a Forge mod, you have to put it in a folder called "mods" inside the "minecraft" folder on your computer. There are two ways to find this folder:

A. Locate it manually by finding the folder at the following location, depending on your operating system:

- **Windows:** C:\Users\You\AppData\Roaming\.minecraft or %AppData%\.minecraft
- **Linux:** ~/.minecraft
- **Mac:** ~/Library/Application Support/minecraf

For Windows, you can open "Run" and simply type "%AppData%\.minecraft" into it, and it will bring it up.

Clicking that "Open resource pack folder" button can help you find the Minecraft folder if you're having a little trouble.

For Mac, open a Finder window, and navigate to the Library folder by holding the "alt" key and clicking "Go" up in the top menu bar. This will show the Library folder as an option; click on that, and then "Application Support," and then "minecraft."

B. Run Minecraft, and go to "Options." Click "Resource Packs," and then "Open resource pack folder." This is easiest done when in "Windowed" mode and not Fullscreen, but either way it will open up the "resource packs" folder in a new window in your operating system. All you have to do then is to go up one folder to the folder "resource packs" is in, and you're in the "minecraft" folder.

3. Move mods into the "mods" folder. In the "minecraft" folder, there should be an empty folder called "mods." If you don't see this, go ahead and create it now. Once you've found it or created it, all you have to do is move the .jar file that you downloaded for each mod into the "mods" folder. Don't open or extract these files, just move them as they are. If the mod file is not a .jar, and is a .zip, you may need to extract the .zip and get the .jar out of it, and then move that over to the "mods" folder.

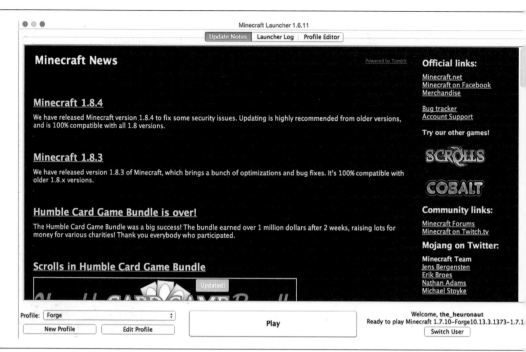

Note the "Forge" profile loaded in the left corner, and the mention of Forge in the right-hand corner as well. This is a Minecraft game that's ready to play some mods!

4. Open the Minecraft launcher and select the Forge profile. When you open the Minecraft launcher, you'll see on the bottom left that there is an option to change which "Profile" you are running. To run mods, you'll need to select and run the Forge profile, which should automatically show up there after you've installed Forge. Note: If you need to, you can click "New Profile" and create a Forge profile yourself. To do this, you'll need to click the "Use version:" dropdown menu and then select the version of Forge you want to run. This can be useful to do if you want to have multiple Forge versions on your computer at once, creating a different profile for each.

5. Check the corner of the launcher. If it says "Ready to play Minecraft" and then something that includes the word "Forge" after it, you're ready to go!

6. Click "Play," and launch Minecraft! If it worked, you will see the regular Minecraft menu (or a new one, depending on the mod), but there will be information in the bottom left hand corner that says Forge is loaded and gives a count of the mods you have running.

7. Start a game! You can usually tell if mods are working by checking the Inventory screen.

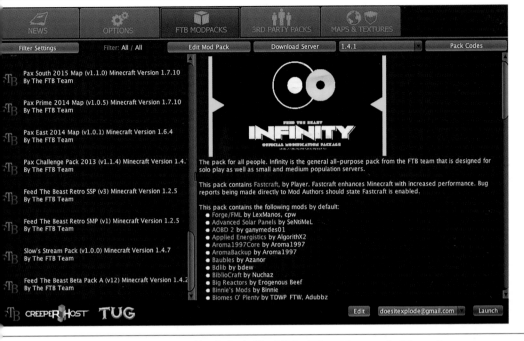

This is what the Feed the Beast mod loader looks like. A little different from regular Minecraft, and it makes loading up complex modpacks a breeze.

OTHER WAYS TO INSTALL MODS

Forge is by far the most commonly used program to run mods, but there are two other ways, the first of which is also pretty well-used by mod players.

1. The Technic and Feed the Beast Launchers: These are two programs that you can use instead of the regular Minecraft launcher, and each makes it very easy to load mods or modpacks. All you have to do is download the file for each launcher, and then open it (only run one at a time, of course) and log into your Minecraft account (the same login you use normally).

There will be a list of mods that you can choose from, and all you have to do to play one is to select it and tell the launcher to "Play" or "Launch." It will then do all of the downloading, installing and launching for you, and should kick you right into the modded game. If something goes wrong, try launching again, and if that doesn't work, head to the Technic or FTB sites to get assistance (they have a lot of people there to help).

This is the Technic loader, another major mod loader with a set of stellar mods and packs to play.

2. Manual installation: Mods can be installed manually without Forge or a launcher, and in fact that's how people used to have to do it before all of these convenient launchers and loaders existed. The instructions to do this are pretty complicated though, and it's easy to mess up your game doing so. If you're interested in doing things the hard way, this is easy to Google, but we highly recommend using one of the more standard ways of installing mods.

MIXING MODS- A FEW TIPS

Some mods are big enough that people often play them on their own, but for the most part, people run more than one mod at the same time. We've touched on this a little bit throughout this chapter, but here are some tips to get the best experience when it comes to mixing mods:

· Always make sure all mods are for the same version of Minecraft.

· Always make sure you are running the correct version of Forge for your mods.

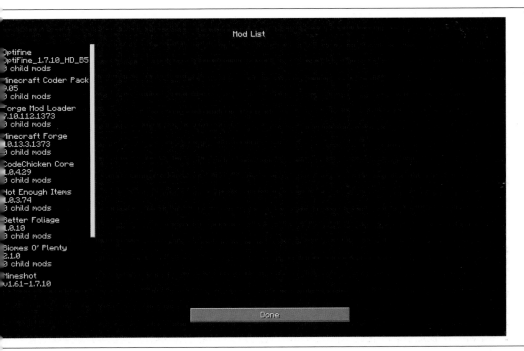

Mod List

Optifine
OptiFine_1.7.10_HD_B5
3 child mods

Minecraft Coder Pack
9.05
3 child mods

Forge Mod Loader
7.10.112.1373
3 child mods

Minecraft Forge
10.13.3.1373
3 child mods

CodeChicken Core
1.0.4.29
3 child mods

Not Enough Items
1.0.3.74
3 child mods

Better Foliage
1.0.10
3 child mods

Biomes O' Plenty
2.1.0
3 child mods

Mineshot
v1.61-1.7.10

Done

When you get mods going and actually get in the game, you can tell which ones loaded in correctly by checking the "Mods" button on the menu, which will get you a big list like this one.

· Install one mod at a time, and run Minecraft between each installation to make sure it works. This will show you which mod is breaking your game if it won't load, something that is very frustrating and tedious to figure out if you have loaded a ton of mods at once.

· Don't overload your computer. Very powerful computers can run a lot of mods at once, but anything less than top-of-the-line models will have trouble the more mods you load in. Keep it at a reasonable level for the kind of machine you have in order to make sure your game runs smoothly.

· Check online for lists of mods that work well together. Many mod creators actually list a few that work well with their mod on their mod's page, and other players have created lists online that go even further.

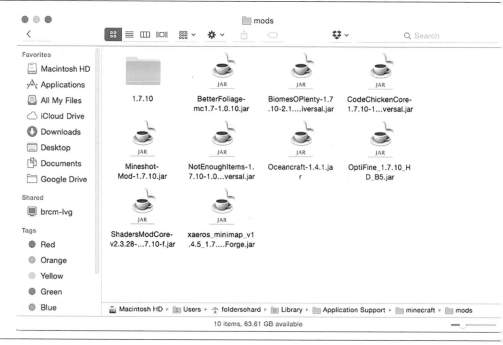

What the mods folder can look like when you get a bunch of mods loaded into it correctly.

TROUBLESHOOTING MODS IN GENERAL

Sometimes a mod just won't work, and there doesn't seem to be a reason why. You can do everything right in installing it, and it can still cause issues in your game or even cause it not to load at all.

This happens, and while each situation will be different, we can give you a few tips for if it happens to you:

- Make sure you know which mod is causing the crash. Remove all other mods and test it alone. If it works alone, it may be conflicting with another mod. If it still doesn't, you know which mod is the culprit.

- Save any information that Minecraft gives you when it crashes. It will usually give a crash report, and may even give an error in the game.

How To Install Your Mods

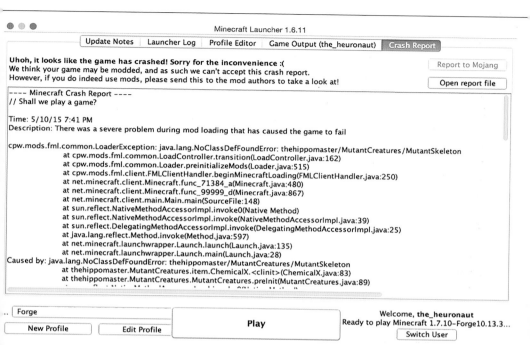

Sometimes mods will crash; that's ok! It happens to everyone, and it usually just means that one or more of your mods are in conflict with another, so you just have to figure out which mods aren't playing well together.

- Check the mod page. Someone else has probably had the same problem you are having, and there is always a lot of discussion on fixes in the comments on Planet Minecraft and the Minecraft Forums. Check there before asking for help.

- Google the problem as well. Sometimes the best troubleshooting discussions are on other pages away from the mod page.

- If you still have trouble, try posting your own request in the Forums. Don't direct message the mod creator though, they tend to hate this and are less likely to get back to you. When you post, make sure to include all information you can about the mod, what version you're trying to run, what computer you are on, what the game said when it crashed and anything else you can think of that might be relevant. Oh, and be nice and patient! People are there to help you, but they won't want to if you are a pest.

Utility **Mods**
Tweaking the Interface and More

Utility Mods are those mods that don't actually add any blocks, biomes, items, mobs, systems, or any other physical changes to the game of Minecraft, but which instead add something to the user interface or otherwise just make the game easier to use and play.

For instance, one of the most popular Utility Mod types is the minimap, which (as you might suspect) adds a little map to the corner of your game, making it much easier to navigate the wild world of Minecraft. Other mods might make finding out information about items easier, or help you find something in the world (like the Horse Locator mod we'll talk about in this chapter).

Most of these mods are very lightweight, meaning they're easy to install, don't change a lot about the game and don't take a lot of computer power to run, and they're all thoroughly useful in their own respective ways. Because of this, Utility Mods are among the most commonly used mods by Minecraft players, and you'll often hear about people using them or find them stuck into modpacks.

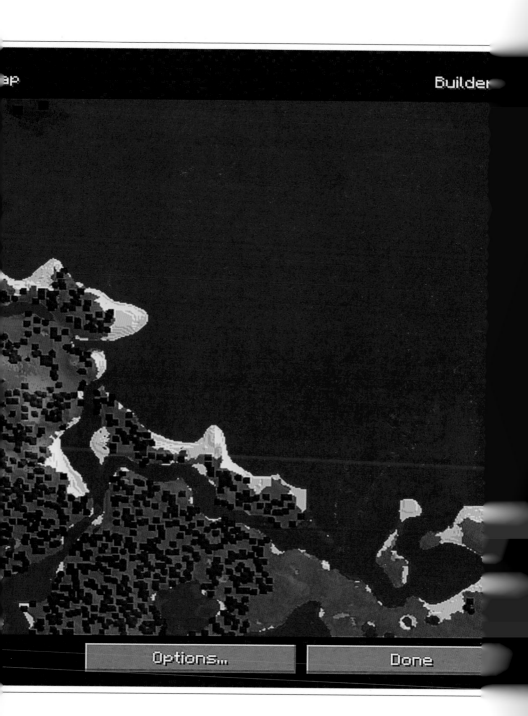

Xaero's Minimap

In one sentence: A cute little pixelated map of the world in the corner of your screen, plus waypoints!

Creator: Xaero
Version: 1.7.10-1.8
Installed Through: Forge (manually)

Where you can find it:
http://bit.ly/XaerosMinimapMod

Complexity Level: 1 Diamond

Mod creator Xaero set out to make a mod that adds a permanent, highly useful map to the corner of your Minecraft screen with the idea that they wanted to make it look more like the rest of Minecraft than most minimap mods. They were quite successful in their efforts, which resulted in the popular and cute Xaero's Minimap mod.

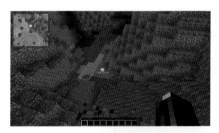

In addition to its Minecraft-y pixelated look, Xaero's Minimap is also tremendously useful. Among its many features are:

· Waypoint creation, to mark anywhere on the map you like

· Map customization, including toggling a grid that shows chunk borders, a zoom, and an orientation lock

· Automatic markers for deathpoints, so you can easily find your way back

· Display of mobs, other players, items

· Easy to read coordinates

· Cave and underground mapping

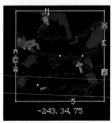

Screenshot: Minecraft® ™ & © 2009–2015 Mojang/Notch

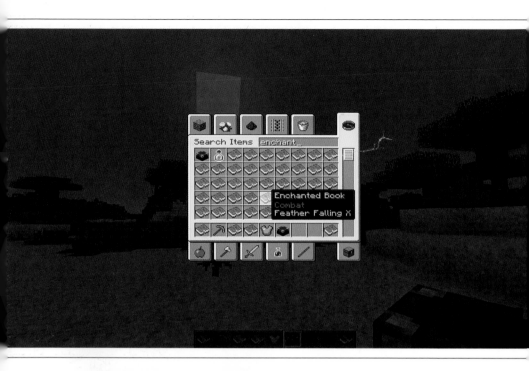

SuperEnchants

In one sentence: Ups the limit on enchanting items to a much higher number than can happen in regular Minecraft.

Creator: Twinklez
Version: 1.7.10
Installed Through: Forge (manually)

Where you can find it:
http://bit.ly/SuperEnchants

Complexity Level: 0.5 Diamonds
Adds Items?: Yes

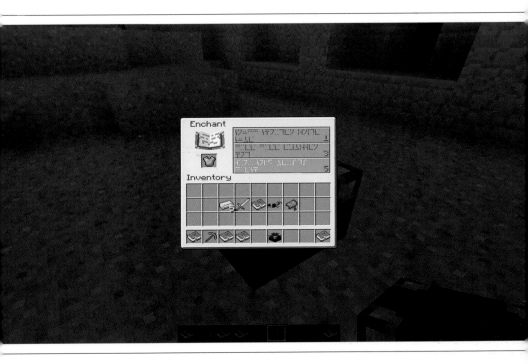

This mod might be considered a system or adventure enhancer, except it's really a quite simple one. Really all it does is to tweak vanilla Minecraft very slightly so that the maximum level of enchants on items is higher. This basically allows you to create items that are quite a good bit more powerful than you can in vanilla Minecraft.

Enchantment level increases:
Increased up to 5-
Sword: Looting, Knockback
Tools: Fortune
Armor: Thorns
Bow: Punch

Increased up to 10-
Sword: Sharpness, Fire Aspect
Tools: Efficiency, Unbreaking
Armor: Protection, Projectile Protection,
Blast Protection, Feather Falling
Bow: Power

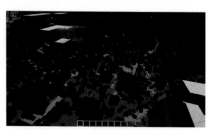

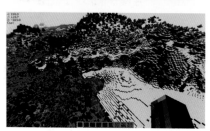

X-Ray Mod

In one sentence: Lets you toggle the ability to see through blocks (whichever ones you want!).

Creator: AmbientOcclusion
Version: 1.6.4-1.8.1
Installed Through: Manually- Forge, LiteLoader, Technic

Where you can find it:
http://bit.ly/XRayModMinecraft

Complexity Level: 1.5 Diamonds

One of the very hardest parts of Minecraft is finding what you need in the wide, confusing worlds you create. Whether it's a special kind of resource, a structure like a cave or a fortress, a mob or another player that's sneaking around, or even your own base (if you got a little lost, as we all can do at times), the X-Ray Mod can help you look right through all the blocks around you to find it.

This mod is toggled on and off with a single key and works very quickly without a lot of drag on your system, and it also can be configured to see through only the blocks you want it to. In other words, if you care about Redstone but don't need Iron right now, you can set this mod to just look for Redstone and to look right through Iron. This can be done to most kinds of blocks, making the X-Ray Mod one of the most powerful tools to save time and energy that's out there. However, using this mod is not okay on all servers, as some consider it cheating. Make sure you use this only on your own worlds or on servers that specifically allow it. No one wants to get the banhammer dropped on their head!

Horse Locator

In one sentence: Finds your horse for you!

Version: 1.7.10
Installed Through: Forge (manually)

Where you can find it:
http://bit.ly/HorseLocator

Complexity Level: 1 Diamond

This mod is for everyone who loves horses in Minecraft, or really just anyone who wants to find one easily. This is a super-lightweight mod that simply adds a little bit of text to the corner of your window to tell you when horses are near. It gives a description of the horse, tells you if it belongs to someone and who, and shows you how far away it is. Once you've actually claimed a horse, you can then use it to find it again no matter where it is. Never lose your horsey pal again!

Horse Locator

Zan's Minimap/ VoxelMap

In one sentence: A highly customizable, very powerful but lightweight mini-map that can show you just about anything you want including mobs and user-set waypoints.

Version: 1.6.4/1.7.10/1.8
Installed Through: Forge (manually)

Where you can find it:
http://bit.ly/VoxelMapLink

Complexity Level: 1.5 Diamonds

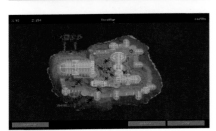

When it comes to minimaps, the VoxelMap (also sometimes known as Zan's minimap) is not only among the most popular, but also the most powerful and customizable. The basic use is that it adds a minimap to the corner of your screen, but it doesn't stop there. You can go into the options for VoxelMap, which also reveals a much larger version of the map (another great feature) and change a huge number of things, including whether it shows mobs (and which kinds, even down to specific mobs) or biomes, has a chunk grid or shows other players, among many other options. You can also change the size and shape, and you can even add named and colored waypoints that will show up both on the big and small map, making it very easy to find things again. This is a beast of a map mod, and it's no surprise that it is very commonly used by Minecraft players.

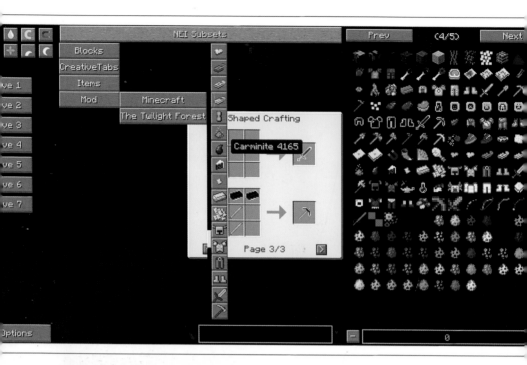

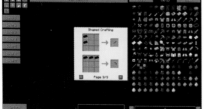

Not Enough Items

In one sentence: A very powerful utility mod that is mostly for gaining information on items (including those from other mods) such as recipes and the like, but which can also do things like save and load inventories, change the weather and time and more.

Version: Pretty much all from 1.8 and back
Installed Through: Forge (manually)
NOTE: You need both the NEI download and the CodeChickenCore file installed in your mods folder for this mod to work

Where you can find it:
http://bit.ly/NotEnoughItemsForum, http://bit.ly/NotEnoughItemsDownloadsPage

Complexity Level: 3 Diamonds

One of the older mods for Minecraft, Not Enough Items, or NEI as it's often called, has been helping players sort, find, use, and understand items for a long time. It was originally created to help sort through the massive amount of items that end up in a Minecraft game that uses a lot of mods, and since then it has developed into one of the most useful and powerful tools for Minecraft that have yet been created. This mod is useful for just about any game (though note that it is mostly a Creative Mode tool) regardless of the number of mods you have though, as it also provides one of the easiest ways to manipulate things like time, weather, and inventories. The ability to press R and click on an item and see its recipe, and to then click on items within that recipe and see what recipes they are used in is tremendously helpful as well, as are the ability to search for an item, to look at items by set type, or to save your inventory. This is a very good one to have in general.

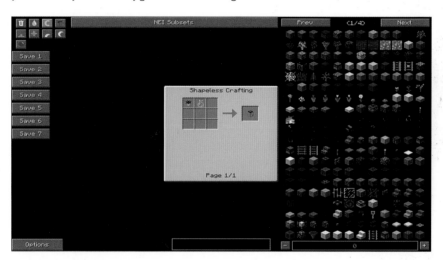

NEI Submod-Waila (What Am I Looking At)

In one sentence: Look at a block, any block, and Waila will give you info on it in a little space at the top of your screen, such as what mod it is from.

Version: 1.7.10/1.8

Installed Through: Forge (manually)

Where you can find it: http://bit.ly/WailaMod

Complexity Level: 0.5 Diamonds

Waila is a mod that is used with Not Enough Items, and it is very simple: install it, and when you point at a block or item, it will give you a little text above the thing you're looking at that tells you what mod it's from. This is very useful when you have a lot of mods running, or when you want to know what stuff works together quickly. Note: there are versions of this that don't require NEI, but it was originally created to work with it.

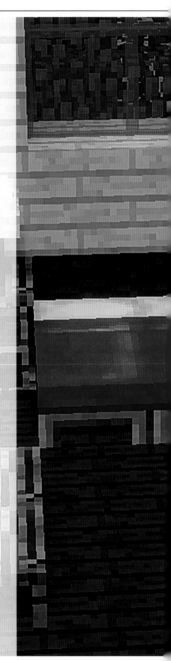

Item **Mods**
More Things, More Fun!

Minecraft is a game built around a few key things: mobs, blocks, and items. In that last category, many different types of items can be found, ranging from those that help the player interact with the world (such as tools and weapons) to those that manipulate other blocks and items in crafting systems, to food, to those that are mostly there for fun and looks.

This chapter deals mostly with those last two categories and the mods that specifically add more food and fun items to the game. This is because most of the mods that add things like new tools and weapons or crafting systems fit better into the categories of Combat mods and Magic, Tech and Crafting Systems, as the mods they come in are more specifically geared toward those subjects.

There are, however, many other mods whose sole purpose is to bring a swarm of new items into the game that aren't predominantly about laying waste to foes or adding in a new, complex crafting system. These mods are more about the items they bring themselves, which serve to add a little flavor, color and aesthetically pleasing attributes to Minecraft builds. Or in the case of the TNT Mod, to give you new ways to blow up all that cute stuff you or someone else built, which is some fun all in itself. Here are seven of the best mods that will give you dozens upon dozens of new items to play around with and use to make your creations more perfectly realized.

Fex's Random Stuff Mod

Creator: FEX___96

In one sentence: Like it says, this mod adds a bunch of random new craftable items, including computers and TVs, robots, food, weapons and a bunch of household stuff.

Version: 1.7.10
Installed Through: Forge (manually)
Where you can find it:
http://fexcraft.net/downloads.html

Complexity Level: 3 Diamonds
Adds Items?: Yes
Adds Mobs?: Sort-of, supposedly has one without a texture

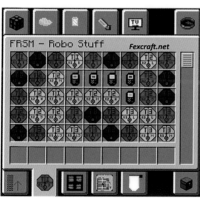

Fex's Random Stuff Mod, or FRSM, has all sorts of items to add to your Minecraft experience, and as the name says, the types of stuff it adds is pretty darn random. Like, for instance, tiny model trains aren't really something that we ever were *looking* to have in Minecraft, but why not!

One of the things FRSM does best is to add a bunch of modern household-style items like TVs, washing machines, computers and a heap of foods like someone might find in their refrigerator. It makes for the ability to really stock up and enliven homes that have a more contemporary look, where before there was definitely a bit of anachronism with modern-looking houses having a bunch of medieval stuff in them.

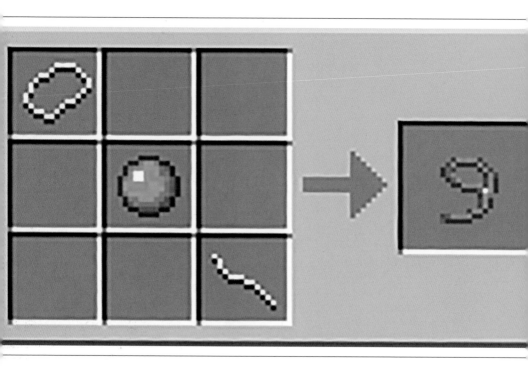

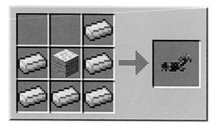

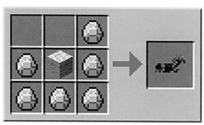

Craftable Horse Armor and Saddles

Creator: SackCastellon

In one sentence: It makes Horse Armor and Name Tags something you can actually craft.

Version: 1.6.1, 1.6.2, 1.6.4, 1.7.2, 1.7.10, 1.8
Installed Through: Forge (manually)
Where you can find it:
http://bit.ly/HorseArmor

Complexity Level: 1.5 Diamonds
Adds Items?: No, just adds crafting options

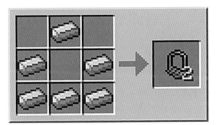

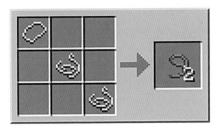

It's always been a bit of a frustration that you can't craft Horse Armor or Name Tags from things- you have to search through the world to find them. This changes that! It's not a big-time mod, and it doesn't add any items, but it does add a thing that really probably should already be a part of Minecraft.

Mr. Crayfish Furniture Mod

Creator: Mr. Crayfish

In one sentence: A mod that's all about decking your home out in furniture, and with an aesthetic that's made to look like it fits right in with regular vanilla Minecraft.

Version: 1.6.4, 1.7.2, 1.7.10
Installed Through: Forge (manually)
Where you can find it:
http://bit.ly/MrCrayfishFurnitureMod

Complexity Level: 2 Diamonds
Adds Items?: Yes

Mr. Crayfish's Furniture Mod consistently ranks in the Top 5 Minecraft mods on the Planet Minecraft page, because it does what it does well, efficiently and in a way that makes it seems like it fits right into regular Minecraft. Many mods add a whole new thing into Minecraft that look out of place in the regular game, which can also be fun, but Mr. Crayfish has done a very good job to make his furniture items have the same look and feel of regular Minecraft items, while greatly expanding what you can add to your home.

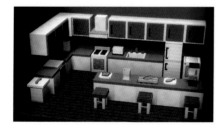

Speaking of what you can add, it's basically everything you'd expect from a regular real-world house, like a fridge, chairs of different types, sinks, blinds, tables, lighting, radios, computers, TVs, and even some weirder stuff like bushes and fire detectors. This is one of those mods that you'll find on a lot of servers, and it's very lightweight, so it's an excellent addition for those wanting to kick their regular home up a notch without changing the game too much.

TNT Mod

Creator: Navist

In one sentence: Adds a massive amount of items designed to help you blow stuff up real nicely, in real big explosions.

Version: 1.7.10
Installed Through: Forge (manually)
Where you can find it:
http://bit.ly/TNTModLink

Complexity Level: 2 Diamonds
Adds Items?: Yes

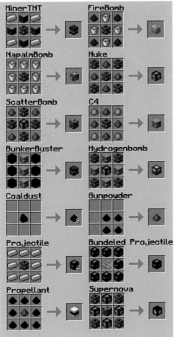

Most of the time when people want to make somethin' go boom in Minecraft, they just stack a whole bunch of TNT together and light it up. That's great and all, but what if you could really make things explode? Like way bigger, and in way more ways?

That most excellent of questions is what the TNT Mod answers, and does so with a huge arsenal of explodey things that are all at the player's disposal. Each explosive does its own thing, whether that means a certain pattern of explosion or a higher or lower level of boom. For instance, you've got the Meteor, which scatters lavabombs, the C4, which is a bit more powerful than regular TNT, and the Nuke TNT, which absolutely obliterates the land. There are also some specialty bombs like the Miner TNT, which causes all exploded blocks to drop so they can be picked up, unlike regular TNT that destroys 70% of blocks.

Party Mod

Creator: TheMCJavaFre4k

In one sentence: The club experience in Minecraft, plus some other party-related items to have an excellent time with your friends!

Version: 1.6.4
Installed Through: Forge (manually)
Where you can find it:
http://bit.ly/PartyMod

Complexity Level: 2 Diamonds
Adds Items?: Yes

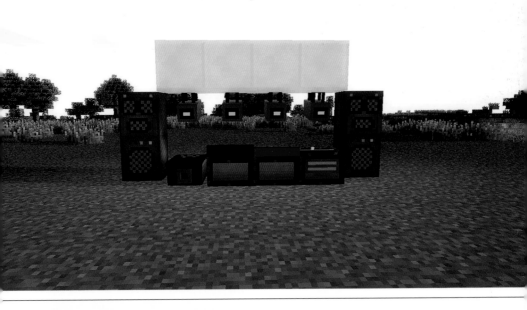

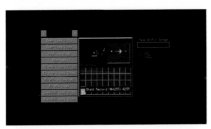

This mod has one use, and one use only, and that's to "Partypartyparty!" as the great Andrew W.K. would say. Everything you need to get down in the virtual world with your friends is here. You've got your DJ decks, your lazers (controllable!), your speakers, your smoke machines, the ability to play songs, and a two-mode color-changing dancefloor to bring it all together. It's a blocky hoedown, danceclub style!

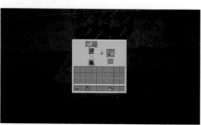

Still Hungry!

Creator: 17CupsofCoffee, DizzyAlyx, and BethW08

In one sentence: A culinary experience inside of Minecraft, adding a new cooking station, cider and beer making and 60+ new food items.

Version: 1.7.2, 1.7.4, 1.7.10
Installed Through: Forge (manually)
Where you can find it: http://bit.ly/StillHungryMod

Complexity Level: 2.5 Diamonds
Adds Items?: Yes

Edibles is another place where vanilla Minecraft chooses simplicity and few options over a more complex system. Still Hungry makes the days of choosing between a few meats, bread, and soup history, adding in not just a grocery store worth of food, but also the options to get complex with your cooking.

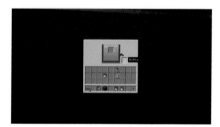

Much of the new gastronomic wonder of this mod comes from a new crafting system for food done through the Stove item added by Still Hungry. It's got a couple slots for combinations of food, which are cooked in Frying Pans or Mugs. Cider and beer can also be concocted with Barrels, which we don't hate one bit. When you're done and ready to head out for the day, you can also take your meal with you in a Lunchbox that stores up to 6 different food items, saving the rest of your valuable inventory space for other cool junk.

Nomnomnom indeed.

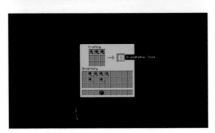

DecoCraft

Creator: ProfMobius, RazzleberryFox, Noppes and the DecoCraft team

In one sentence: Brings a set of items called "Deco Clay" into the game, with which you can craft many different decorative items.

Version: 1.6.4, 1.7.2, 1.7.10
Installed Through: Forge (manually) or through the Technic Pack
Where you can find it:
bit.ly/DecoCraftModLink

Complexity Level: 2.5 Diamonds
Adds Items?: Yes

Quirky and cute is the name of the game with the DecoCraft mod which is chock full of items that fit that description, most of which are meant to lend your home a little fun and personality. There are objects for both indoors (beds, toys, lighting, plumbing, decorations etc.) and outdoors (signs, things to make a park, outdoor decorations), and all of them are crafted using various combinations of different colors of Deco Clay.

The Deco folks take decoration in the game to new heights, and are also quite good at utilizing their own creations on their server, where they have built some great spaces nicely filled with the Deco items.

Land & Biome Design **Mods**
A Better View

Minecraft's many biomes are lovely, excitin' places to get your dig-and-build on, but after a little while exploring the swamps, mesas, forests, deserts, and more that vanilla 'Craft has to offer, you do start to wonder what the world of Minecraft would be like if it was just a little more varied.

Enter the land and biome design mods, whose sole purpose is to take that vanilla landscape and turn it into something more complex, varied and simply awesome. These mods run the gamut from those that add new biomes into Minecraft that generate the same way the regular ones do, but contain a different, new set of plants and an all-new look, to those that change the land in more specific ways, such as adding new features to existing biomes. There's even one that plants a dang new dimension right into your vanilla world, which essentially acts like a separate, magical biome replete with its own flora and fauna that's accessed by a secret portal! It's, quite literally, a whole new world out there with land and biome design mods, and it's just waiting for you to load it up and step into it.

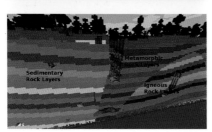

Mineralogy

Creator: DrCyrano

In one sentence: Instead of having just random bits of Stone, Dirt, Gravel and ores scattered through the underground portion of your Minecraft world, Mineralogy causes rock and soil layers to spawn in Minecraft similarly to how they do in real life.

Version: 1.7.10, 1.8
Installed Through: Forge (manually)
Where you can find it:
http://bit.ly/MineralogyMod,
https://github.com/cyanobacterium/
Minecraft_Mineralogy

Complexity Level: 2 Diamonds
Adds Items?: Yes
Adds Mobs?: No

In places like the Grand Canyon, you can visibly see that the world is not just large chunks of the same kind of rock or material, but instead it's made of layers of various types of materials that are set one on top of the other. It's pretty cool looking, and it is also the inspiration for the real-world replication Mineralogy mod for Minecraft. This mod does two things that are meant to simulate the way the real world ground-stuff works: first, it adds a large amount of new types of rock and ground materials, and second, it layers those materials in a very realistic way.

This includes not just layers, but actually the various types of layers, which run into each other at different angles. In the real world, this is because of different types of rock pushing up from various parts of the inside of the earth running into each other (such as igneous rocks from volcano and inner-earth activity running into sedimentary rock layers), and that's what Mineralogy is designed to simulate. It might be a little technical, but we think it's very cool, and it also looks pretty darn sweet.

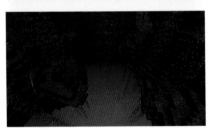

Biomes o' Plenty

Creator: Glitchfiend

In one sentence: New biomes, and plenty of 'em, even in the Nether!

Version: 1.6.4-1.8
Installed Through: Forge (manually)
Where you can find it:
http://bit.ly/BiomesOPlentyMod

Complexity Level: 2 Diamonds
Adds Items?: Yes
Adds Mobs?: No

75 new biomes. Yep, that is not a typo, this mod adds 75 entire new biomes to your vanilla Minecraft world. That's 75 new biomes to play in, dig up, and build giant bases in, and many of 'em have a whole new set of plants and materials to turn into cool new stuff. It's a veritable smorgasbord of plants and pretty landscapes. It's especially spectacular with shader mods, and for those of you who are all about the exploration, the Next Horizon style Crafters, this is the one you want. It even goes so far as to add a bunch of neat stuff to the Nether which, let's face it, could use a facelift.

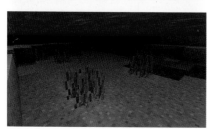

ExtrabiomesXL

Creator: ExtrabiomesXL Team

In one sentence: Another mod with a plethora of very well-designed biomes run by a team thoroughly committed to creating the best mod it can.

Version: 1.5.2, 1.7.10
Installed Through: Forge (manually)
Where you can find it:
http://bit.ly/ExtrabiomesXLMod

Complexity Level: 2 Diamonds
Adds Items?: Yes
Adds Mobs?: No

The team behind ExtrabiomesXL is among the best when it comes to taking what it does seriously and really giving the community of modders something amazing. This mod is another that simply adds a ton of great biome content to vanilla 'Craft, with over 25 painstakingly designed and well-updated biomes to give your Minecraft world a little more ecological oomph. The folks working on this have really done their research on environments, and it comes across in their work with excellent generation algorithms for environs like marshes, redwood forests, and the rocky alpine biome.

The Twilight Forest

Creator: Benimatic

In one sentence: A new, fantastical dimension of glimmering dusk adventures through a magical forest, complete with fascinating creatures, an adventure to follow and all manner of new plants and blocks to discover.

Version: 1.7.10 and way back
Installed Through: Forge (manually) or through the FTB Launcher
Where you can find it:
http://bit.ly/TwilightForestPage

Complexity Level: 3.5 Diamonds
Adds Items?: Yes
Adds Mobs?: Yes

The Twilight Forest mod is one of our very favorites, as it is just so darn enchanting. As opposed to other biome mods, this one is not just randomly created in the world; you actually have to build a portal to it and jump in. Once you do that, you'll find yourself surrounded by what might be the most aesthetically wonderful realm in all of modded Minecraft, with its own set of biomes and areas, not to mention unique mobs and things to experience. It truly is the premier fantasy environment in Minecraft, and it feels like you just stepped into the pages of a 1970s fantasy adventure novel, or the land of the movie *Legend*.

Once you do step into this perpetual twilight land, you'll notice immediately that everything is different. Deer and Fireflies and Bighorns roam the land, and the towering trees are not even a bit like the ones from regular Minecraft. There is also much to fear in this new world, which will throw over a dozen new hostile mobs at you, such as the Kobold and Swarm Spider or bosses like the Naga, Hydra, and Lich.

There is a bit of an RPG element to the story of this land, as well as to its aesthetic, as it is set up to have a progression from boss to boss, and the land itself is designed to draw you through these progressions. Along the way you'll find well over a hundred new blocks and items to mine, manipulate, craft and master, all with a fantasy bent and totally fun to discover. It is a beautiful place and a beautiful mod, and it's one every Crafter who has ever been interested in fantasy should check out.

OceanCraft

Creator: thomassu

In one sentence: Utterly transforms the ocean biome into a much more dynamic place, full of life and with many new craft-ready blocks, plus an overhauled generation system.

Version: 1.5.2, 1.6.4, 1.7.2, 1.7.10
Installed Through: Forge (manually)
Where you can find it:
http://bit.ly/OceanCraftModLink

Complexity Level: 2.5 Diamonds
Adds Items?: Yes
Adds Mobs?: Yes

The Oceancraft mod could easily fit into the Mobs or Adventure Enhancer chapters, because it adds so many creatures and general things to experience to your game, but because it is so biome-centric, and it also heavily manipulates the spawning of that biome, it fits best here in this book. Oceancraft is the beach-lover's dream come true in Minecraft, taking the regular, pretty boring seascape of the game and making it much more like the real beach.

The life of the ocean is a major part of this mod, with Crabs, Orcas, Sea Turtles and all manner of ocean-faring mobs added, and it doesn't shirk the plantlife either, adding a wide variety of water fauna. Coral is also a big part of this mod, being a new craftable material in the vein of ores, allowing for armor and tools to be made of its pink porous self. Speaking of items, Oceancraft has many, all sticking to its oceanic theme.

Oceancraft even adds new generated structures and land, from the way the floor of the sea looks itself to new ground structures near it, such as the huts of the Beachvillager. While this mod is by no means the most extensive or comprehensive mod, it does manage to massively enhance one very particular biome in a way few other mods do, and it makes it heaps more fun to live by the sea in Minecraft.

Combat
Mods
Turning the Fights
Up a Notch

Minecraft is a rare game in that combat is more a side thing and not the main focus of the game, but that is really only true in vanilla Minecraft. Even in plain ole 'Craft, people do get up to quite a lot of bashin' and smashin', and if you go to just about any online server, the amount of battling you do goes up quite a large amount. Even though Minecraft isn't really built around combat, people have come up with some really awesome ways to do PvP in this game, and have gotten really good at it, and in no part of the game is that more true than when it comes to mod-aided Minecraft combat.

Combat mods come in a lot of shapes and sizes, from those that just add a few little weapons, to those that deal more with helping you get more information about combat, to those that totally overhaul the whole weapons and fighting systems. Here, you'll find all of these types, as we've collected a group of mods that represent the best of the combat mods available today.

Screenshot: Minecraft® ™ & © 2009–2015 Mojang/Notch

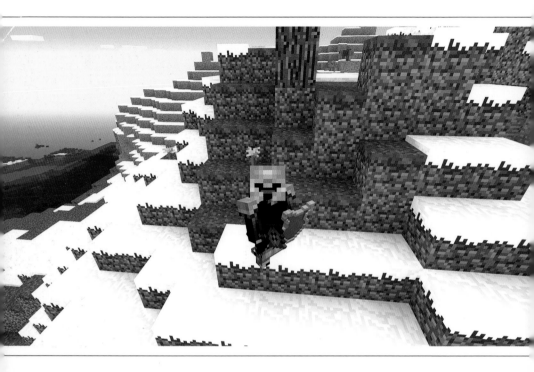

Mine and Blade Battlegear 2

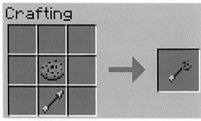

Creator: Full Stack

In one sentence: Expands the weapons system in Minecraft significantly, including not only new weapons, but also the ability to use two at once, save weapon configurations and even use shields.

Version: 1.5.2-1.7.10 (1.8 upcoming, according to the forum page)
Installed Through: Forge (manually)
Where you can find it:
http://bit.ly/MineandBlade2

Complexity Level: 2 Diamonds
Adds Items?: Yes
Adds Mobs?: No

Combat Mods

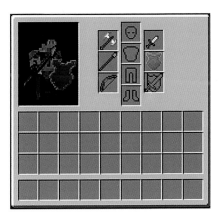

Actually called Mine and Blade Battlegear 2 for this version, this is a Modpack that is named after the war simulation battle game Mount & Blade and which adds a very large amount of things to kill other Crafters and mobs with to your game. That is to say, it's chock full of weapons! While many Modpacks add weapons, Mine and Blade is considered one of the best, and it even adds the ability to use a shield and dual-wield some killing implements. And like many mods, Mine and Blade adds quite a lot of new craftable items, like the expensive but deadly Diamond Arrow. It also gives Crafters the ability to save weapon configurations in its new inventory set-up so they can easily switch between various implements, and it has an extra little feature that tells you if there is a new version of Mine & Blade out automatically, which is quite helpful.

Better PvP

Creator: xaero96

In one sentence: Gives you stats and other information on combat and combat-related things through the user interface, plus Xaero's minimap and some handy tweaks to make things like running and eating food much easier.

Version: 1.7.10, 1.8
Installed Through: Forge (manually)
Where you can find it:
http://bit.ly/BetterPVP

Complexity Level: 1.5 Diamonds
Adds Items?: No
Adds Mobs?: No

This might be considered a utility mod, if it weren't so specifically for use in combat. Better PvP is designed to give you much, much more information on combat situations than you would normally have. Better PvP adds info like weapon and armor status, potion effects, Arrow counts, and enchantment statuses, as well as giving indicators of quick combat events, such as when you're being shot by arrows, when you gain or lose XP, or when something is about to explode near you. Additionally, this thing will cut down on your need to jump in and out of inventory or use inefficient button combinations in combat by giving you options like binding food eating to a certain key or making sprinting much easier.

And to sweeten the deal, Xaero includes his very good little minimap (which you can find on its own in our Utility Mods chapter) with Better PvP, which is highly useful in combat both for its ability to show the enemies and land around and for its feature that shows you where your last death occurred. All in all, an immensely useful combat mod which doesn't actually change the way combat works in vanilla Minecraft by adding items or new systems.

Paintball Mod

Creator: IKinx

In one sentence: Play paintball in Minecraft with a variety of weapons and equipment like flags and base creators that create a minigame similar to real-life paintball.

Version: 1.6.2 through 1.8
Installed Through: Forge (manually)
Where you can find it:
http://bit.ly/PaintballMod

Complexity Level: 2 Diamonds
Adds Items?: Yes
Adds Mobs?: No

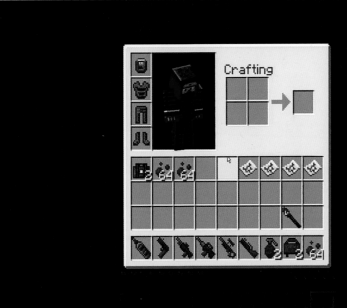

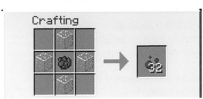

If you've ever played real-life paintball with a good crew of friends at the right paintball place (and a bit of pain doesn't phase you), you know that the excitement and camaraderie and chaos can be just a huge amount of fun. Mod creator IKinx (who is looking to make a career of this, so make sure to support them if you can!) has brought this very thrill to our favorite building game with the awesome Paintball Mod, which features everything you need to get a game going. This includes a huge number of weapon types (pistols, sniper rifles, machine guns, shotguns, grenades and more), as well as ammo and items to set up your gameplay area, like automatic base creators and flags. All of this is craftable, and IKinx has conveniently provided downloads for server-side mod stuff on his site as well, if you have your own server goin'.

Ferullo's Guns Mod

Creator: Ferullo

In one sentence: Another old one, this is perhaps the primary gun-adding mod for Minecraft, adding many realistic guns to the game.

Version: 1.6.4
Installed Through: Forge (manually)
Where you can find it:
http://bit.ly/FerullosGunsMod

Complexity Level: 2 Diamonds
Adds Items?: Yes
Adds Mobs?: No

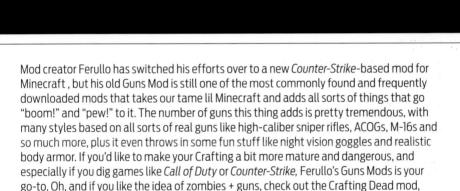

Mod creator Ferullo has switched his efforts over to a new *Counter-Strike*-based mod for Minecraft , but his old Guns Mod is still one of the most commonly found and frequently downloaded mods that takes our tame lil Minecraft and adds all sorts of things that go "boom!" and "pew!" to it. The number of guns this thing adds is pretty tremendous, with many styles based on all sorts of real guns like high-caliber sniper rifles, ACOGs, M-16s and so much more, plus it even throws in some fun stuff like night vision goggles and realistic body armor. If you'd like to make your Crafting a bit more mature and dangerous, and especially if you dig games like *Call of Duty* or *Counter-Strike*, Ferullo's Guns Mods is your go-to. Oh, and if you like the idea of zombies + guns, check out the Crafting Dead mod, which uses this Guns Mod, but adds in a whole zombie apocalypse thing (find it in our Technic Launcher chapter)!

Mob **Mods**
More Friends and More Foes

Every time Mojang releases a new mod with a Minecraft update, it's a big ole deal, and everyone goes crazy about the new creature roaming the lands of Minecraft. What modded Minecraft players know that those who just play vanilla might not, however, is that you can have that feeling times thirty or so all at once, right now!

Mob mods (it's fun to say, isn't it?) are some of the most requested things that Minecraft players getting into the modding scene ask for, and that makes a lot of sense, as adding even one new creature into the game really does liven it up a big amount. Luckily, mod creators have gone out there and added just about every imaginable creature to Minecraft and jammed them all into mods that are among the easiest to install and the least likely to mess up your existing worlds. If you're lookin' for a few new friends to hang out with (or enemies to slay!), one or two of the mods in this chapter will set you right.

Mutant Creatures

Creator: thehippomaster21

In one sentence: Turns regular mobs into weird, bigger, way more dangerous versions of themselves.

Version: 1.7.10 and back
Installed Through: Forge (manually)
Where you can find it:
http://bit.ly/MutantCreaturesMCMod,
http://bit.ly/MutantCreatures1710Download

Complexity Level: 1.5 Diamonds
Adds Items?: No
Adds Mobs?: Changes mobs, but doesn't add

Ever looked at an Enderman and thought, "Enderman, you just aren't weird enough!" With the Mutant Creatures mod, it's unlikely you'll be doing that ever again, as its whole premise is to take the plain versions of mobs and seriously weird them up. Mobs get bigger, really freaky lookin', and have much more strength and better attacks. In a fun twist, this mod also allows you to create minion Creepers, which will attempt to aid you against the mutants' onslaught by blowin' them right up. Watch out though- they might get overexcited and accidentally catch you in the explosion too!

Doggy Talents

Creator: ProPercivalalb

In one sentence: Massively expands what your pet Dog can do in Minecraft, especially adding a huge number of "talents" you can train your dog in, such as hunting and herding.

Version: 1.8 and down
Installed Through: Forge (manually)
Where you can find it:
http://bit.ly/DoggyTalentsMod

Complexity Level: 2 Diamonds
Adds Items?: Yes
Adds Mobs?: Changes mobs, but doesn't add

Taming a Wolf and getting your very own trusty puppy is one of the cuter, more cuddly things you can do in Minecraft, but let's be honest: the Dogs in vanilla Minecraft don't really do much. No longer, with the Doggy Talents mod! This thing is pretty lightweight, but surprisingly complex, and it really does turn your furry pal into a hugely useful friend. The way it works is that you craft special treats for your Dog and feed them to him or her to train them, which levels them up. Each time they level up, you can spend points in a massive variety of different talents, which include everything from making them move faster, have poison attacks, herd peaceful mobs and much more. This mod also allows you to name your pet, which shows up above their head, to tell your pet how to behave (such as to attack everything in sight or only what you tell it to), and it even adds special Dog items like beds and baths. This is the ideal mod for everyone who loves their digital pet and wants to make their relationship with it even stronger.

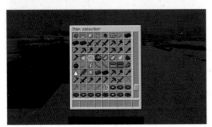

More Mobs Mod

Creator: SimJoo

In one sentence: All the mobs you could ever want, including new human mobs, and some neat items like Wings.

Version: 1.7.2, 1.7.10
Installed Through: Forge (manually)
Where you can find it:
http://bit.ly/MoreMobsmod

Complexity Level: 2 Diamonds
Adds Items?: Yes
Adds Mobs?: Oh yes

This is the big one when it comes to adding new types of mobs to your Minecraft world, as it features well over 30 new mobs of all different shapes, sizes, and types. It also adds a few neat new craftable items like Fire tools and Wings, which make it a double whammy of a mod. Primarily though, this is mostly a big-time mob mod, and the list of the mobs this mod adds reads like a zoo directory. Check it out:

ANIMALS:
Dog (different from trained Wolf)
Zebra
Rabbit (different from vanilla)
Hedgehog
Lion
Penguin
Swamp Crawler
Goat
Bee

NETHER MOBS:
Evil Steve
Reaper
Lava
Lava Snake

END MOBS:
Sprender
Crender
EnderPig
Endead
EnderCube
EndPC
Skelender

HUMANS:
Priest
Knight
Lumberjack
Merchant
New Villager

MONSTERS:
Ghosts (Orange/Purple)
Dark Zombie
Ent
Creep
Burning Obsidian

Mystical Creatures

Creator: FiskFile

In one sentence: An older but highly unique mob mod that adds new mobs that are mutant combinations of two mods already in the game.

Version: 1.6.4
Installed Through: Forge (manually)
Where you can find it:
http://bit.ly/MysticalCreatures

Complexity Level: 1.5
Adds Items?: Yes
Adds Mobs?: Yes

This is another one for older versions of the game, but we included it because it's just freakishly adorable and fun. Mystical Creatures can be thought of as loosely based around what would happen if an accident caused mobs in the Minecraft world to merge, creating all new, kinda horrifying creatures. For instance, it has the Cow and Squid merged into a crossbreed that is both ridable and can be milked to get Calamari Stew, and the Spider/Creeper that can climb, jump on your head and blow up. The other two mobs added are the Enderman/Skeleton and the Morbid Harvester (kind of a mash up of the Spider and Enderman), and these last two drop Enderman Scales (to make armor) and the Morbid Harvester Arm (a powerful weapon), respectively.

Mythical Creatures

Creator: HurricaneSHLBHP

In one sentence: A creature mod that adds all manner of fun, fantastical creatures like dragons, crocodiles and some ponies you might recognize, as well as some item additions like extra-long swords and enchanted armor.

Version: 1.6.4
Installed Through: Forge (manually)
Where you can find it:
http://bit.ly/MythicalCreaturesMod

Complexity Level: 2 Diamonds
Adds Items?: Yes
Adds Mobs?: Yes

This mod doesn't mess around with systems or anything fancy, but in terms of the kinds of mods it adds, it's the most imaginative on this list. It's all fantasy stuff here, turning your Minecraft world into a land of mythical (thus the name!) and quite dangerous beasts. Plus, you get the fun addition of some cool items to play around with, including, as they say on their forum page "stuff that can cause ridiculously huge explosions." This is another good one for when you don't want to add in anything too complex, you just want to make your existing world a little more flavorful.

Mythical Creatures

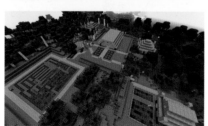

Millénaire

Creator: Kinniken

In one sentence: Adds five new types of Villages to Minecraft, each of which has its own culture and an extensive amount of new items and Villager types, and which can grow, trade and interact with the player in a large number of ways.

Version: 1.7.2, 1.7.10
Installed Through: Forge (manually) or through the Millénaire mod installer
Where you can find it:
http://millenaire.org/

Complexity Level: 3.5 Diamonds
Adds Items?: Yes
Adds Mobs?: Yes

The basic idea of Millénaire is simple, but in actuality this is one of the more complex and comprehensive mods out there, so much so that it would almost be a total conversion mod if it weren't otherwise set in vanilla Minecraft. The core concept is that there are various cultures of Villagers around the Minecraft world in randomly generated Villages, and these Villagers all have jobs like mining or chopping Wood (instead of just milling about). There is a leader, a trading hall and there are many ways to interact with the Villages, including helping them get items they need to build their Village and taking quests from them.

On top of this, you can also gain a reputation with these Villages and even become a leader, which in turn allows you the option to build your own Village that you can control (in terms of what they do and build). The Creation Quest you can get from the Villages is also a pretty big change to the game, as it adds in a little backstory for the Minecraft world and sends the player on an epic quest to gather items and information. All-in-all, Millénaire is a way to really spice up and populate the regular Minecraft world, turning it into more of an RPG builder game with a plot and characters, as opposed to being just about what the player wants to do. It's very cool, and one of the best ways to bring excitement back into the game if you're a little bored with regular Crafting.

Minecraft Comes Alive

Creator: WildBamaBoy and SheWolfDeadly

In one sentence: Another Villager mod, but this one is more about tweaking existing Villagers so they can be more intricately interacted with and so that they look and behave in a wider variety of ways.

Version: 1.6.4, 1.7.2, 1.7.10
Installed Through: Forge (manually), requires both MCA and the RadixCore
Where you can find it:
http://www.radix-shock.com/
mca--overview.html, http://bit.ly/
MinecraftComesAliveCurse"

Complexity Level: 3 Diamonds
Adds Items?: Yes
Adds Mobs?: Yes

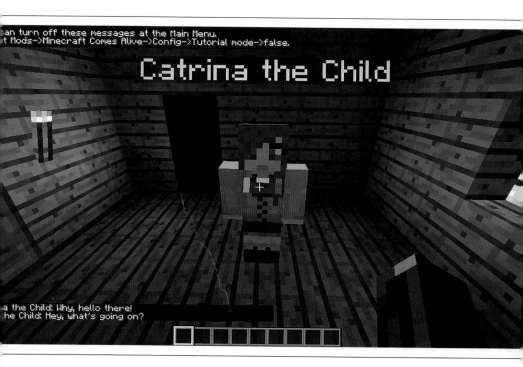

Villagers are loud, annoying, almost useless little creatures in vanilla Minecraft (okay, they're pretty adorable too), and it always seems like you should be able to interact with them a lot more than you can. Where Millénaire is all about economy and interacting with Villagers on a bigger scale, Minecraft Comes Alive is about Villager personalities and having relationships with them. It replaces the strange-nosed, squawking brown Villager models that don't do much with a whole heap of Villager skins (about 200 of them!) that are much more human, and it changes the shape of Villages to be much more realistic.

Even better, you can now click on Villagers and interact with them in dozens of ways, including flirting, talking and even hiring them to do jobs! Each Villager has its own specialization, like farming or guarding, and its own personality, and they remember your interactions with them. You can become friends or, if you get close enough, even marry one. There are literally thousands of dialogue options with Villagers in Minecraft Comes Alive, and while it's not the world-changer that Millénaire is, it's probably the best semi-vanilla Minecraft mod for Villagers out there.

Building
Mods
Quick Buildings
& More

Building is awesome, but sometimes it's not really what you want to spend time on in Minecraft. Say you want to get into some combat, or do some exploring of a new mod- having to sit and build a whole home, or using a very basic, crappy home really aren't great options.

That's why there are convenient quick-building mods out there, like the two we're showing off in this chapter. They essentially do the same thing in two different ways for two different reasons, that being that they allow you to very, very quickly spawn pre-built structures of different types right into your world without having to do any of the work.

Note: Technically, many of the mods in the rest of our book deal with building, such as those that add new block types, but we consider those to be more crafting and general mods. The mods here are more about making building faster and easier, as opposed to giving you more objects to build with. For those types of mods, check out the Items and the Adventure Enhancer chapters, along with a few other mods scattered throughout our book.

Instant Structures Mod

Creator: MaggiCraft

In one sentence: Spawn all sorts of different structures into your Minecraft world with just one click, or spawn different sized chunks of blocks.

Version: 1.7.10, 1.8
Installed Through: Forge (manually)
Where you can find it:
http://bit.ly/InstantStructuresForum

Complexity Level: 2.5 Diamonds
Adds Items?: No
Adds Mobs?: No

Building Mods

Over 170 different structures of various sizes and types are packed into this mod, whose goal is to help players speed up creation in their own worlds. Whether you just want a quick medieval windmill in your city and don't want to have to design one yourself, or you have found the perfect spot for a house and need one quick, the Instant Structures Mod has you covered. The selection of available structures is staggering, including everything from entire cities, to boats of all shapes and styles, to a ton of houses and generic buildings, to even statues, pixel art, a huge number of vehicles and so much more.

Perhaps even more awesome, this mod also includes a feature that allows you to spawn custom-sized shapes of different kinds, like pyramids and spheres, or remove blocks in an area. And the icing on the cake is that this feature also lets you scan your own structures into its system, allowing you to replicate them wherever you wish! It is a triumph of quick building, and a great mod for those who are looking to cut a few corners.

Instant Massive Structures Mod

Creator: SimJoo

In one sentence: Add a variety of simple structures into your Minecraft world with a single click, as opposed to the highly complex builds of MaggiCraft's mod.

Version: 1.6.4, 1.7.2, 1.7.10
Installed Through: Forge (manually)
Where you can find it:
bit.ly/InstantMassiveStructures

Complexity Level: 2 Diamonds
Adds Items?: No
Adds Mobs?: No

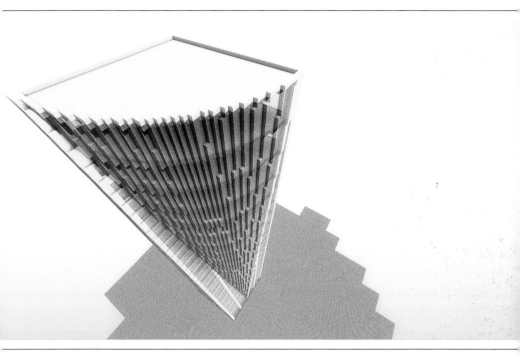

While the Instant Structures Mod is great, its builds are pretty much the kind of thing you'd see as complete builds on a server or as a downloadable map. That's great, but it doesn't allow for much customization, as they're already pretty much done. If you're looking more for something that will add simple structures that you can then tweak and build on, turning them into your own creation, this is the building mod you want.

Now, that isn't to say that the builds in this mod are all just utterly simple. There are some quite nicely designed buildings and vehicles in here as well, such as a very well-done tower. However, the idea here is to keep things more simple and leave space for the user to create their own thing out of them, and that makes it one of the most useful mods there is when it comes to speeding up building.

Adventure Enhancers
Mods That Give You More To Do On Your Journey

Outside of building things, adventure and fantastical experiences are what Minecraft is all about. Though some players choose to spend all their time crafting, mining and perfecting their home, which is also great fun, there are those of us who feel the itch to gear up and head out into the wilderness each time we see the sun rise over those virtual mountains in the distance.

You never know what will be over that next rise, what creatures or land features await, and one of Minecraft's best qualities is its ability to make you say "Whoa, come check this out!"

That's what this chapter is all about: mods that add more of those "Whoa" adventuring moments to your game. Many of these mods could fit in other chapters in this book, as they often add mobs, items, biomes, systems and just about everything else we've talked about, but we've given them a special category because these mods almost all add more than one of those things, and some even add all of them.

Additionally, the focus of these mods is more about directing your overall Minecraft experience in a certain direction, such as injecting an ancient Egyptian adventure into your game (Atum), making survival more realistic and difficult (TerrafirmaCraft) or turning dungeons into huge, mightily challenging structures (Chocolate Quest, Roguelike Dungeons). They are, each one, an adventure in themselves, and they will enhance the fun, magic, and wonder of the overall journey in your Minecraft world tremendously.

The Aether 2

Creators: Brandon "Kingbdogz" Pearce and Emile van Krieke

In one sentence: Adds a sky dimension that's basically the counterpart to the Nether, with a light, happy and airy aesthetic instead of a hellish one.

Version: Automatic

Installed Through: Aether Launcher or Forge (also requires Guilded Games Utility)
Where you can find it:
http://bit.ly/Aether2Link

Complexity Level: 3 Diamonds
Adds Items?: Yes
Adds Mobs?: Yes

The Aether mod adds a new dimension to your world that is the polar opposite of the Nether. The Aether
is a sky dimension, and it keeps with that theme by including flying animals (Pigs with wings!), lots of cloud- based items and a very fluffy and light look and feel. It's also a huge challenge, however, as it adds in three neat little Aether dungeons that have dangerous mobs and bosses in them, and each of which has a reward.

It's a quite enduringly popular Minecraft mod, both for its look and for the fact that it's just very well done. As opposed to many mods, The Aether feels at once complete, complex, and perfectly at home in the world of Minecraft, and though it does add a very big number of new items, block types and mobs, all of that stuff can only be picked up or seen in The Aether itself, meaning that the rest of your Minecraft world will stay the same. This makes it feel like just a really big update to the regular game, as opposed to mods that make Minecraft feel like a totally different game (though that's fun too!).

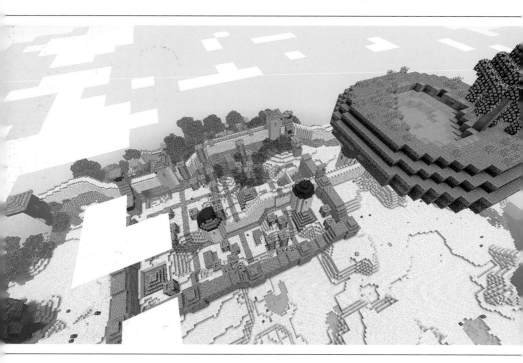

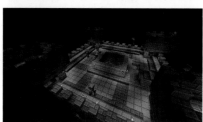

Crusader Craft

Creator: The VoidsWrath team

In one sentence: Have a *Lord of the Rings/* medieval themed adventure in this huge, very immersive mod with tons of items, characters, locations, and new systems.

Version: 1.7.10
Installed Through: The VoidLauncher (follow link below)
Where you can find it:
http://bit.ly/CrusaderMod

Complexity Level: 4.5 Diamonds
Adds Items?: Yes
Adds Mobs?: Yes

Adventure Enhancers

Frankly, this mod is the *Lord of the Rings* experience we've been dreaming of in our most feverish, Gandalf-lovin' nerd dreams. This modpack is all about living in Middle Earth (though in its most recent incarnations they have made the distinction that it is not all LOTR stuff), and you can explore the whole realm, from Hobbiton all the way to fiery Mordor. The gameplay is as off-rails as can be, meaning no one's sitting there forcing you to go kick Uruk Hai butt, and if you want to save the realm, you gotta step away from the elevensies table and get to it yourself.

You'll have to figure out how to open the portal to the land of *Lord of the Rings* by exploring another medieval world and collecting the necessary items to create the portal, at which point you'll be teleported to a giant land literally the entire size of Middle Earth as it is in the books and films.

This modpack is absolutely huge, with well over 40 separate mods included that run the gamut from the implementation of magic (the beloved Ars Magica mod) to a new set of monsters to a whole adventuring system based on the monumental fantasy series. This is one of those mods that outright changes everything about your Minecraft experience, and it's not to be slept on by fantasy fans.

Galacticraft

Creator: micdoodle8

In one sentence: Craft through all new systems to build, launch and fly a rocket, going all the way to the moon and Mars!

Version: 1.7.10 and back to 1.4.7
Installed through: Forge (manually), and is also in many modpacks
Where you can find it:
http://bit.ly/GalacticraftMod

Complexity Level: 4.5 Diamonds
Adds Items?: Yes
Adds Mobs?: Yes

Included in many modpacks (such as A Era do Futuro), Galacticraft deserves its own section because what it does is just so darn cool: it lets you build a rocketship and go to space! SPACE! In actuality, Galacticraft is a lot more than that, adding entire new systems and hundreds of new items and block-types to the game, all of which have a high-tech, sci-fi kind of theme to them.

The "space" you go to in Galacticraft is pretty awesome too, being basically three new dimensions that you can travel to and build in. These include the Moon (no longer just a bunch of pixels hanging in the sky, but an actual place you can fly to and stand on!), the space around the earth (meant to be as if you're in orbit, and you can build space stations there) and Mars. If you fire this mod up and are lookin' to take a rocket up to see what you can find, however, make sure you bring a spacesuit, as even virtual space doesn't have a whole lot of air for your character to breathe!

(Though excellent on its own, we'd suggest grabbing Galacticraft in Technic's Tekkit modpack, which is made to make Galacticraft even better by adding other cool mods.

Roguelike Dungeons

Creator: Greymerk

In one sentence: Takes inspiration from dungeon crawler roguelike games and causes Minecraft to generate extensive, interesting dungeons full of mob spawners and a ton of cool stuff.

Version: 1.6.4, 1.7.2, 1.7.10, 1.8
Installed Through: Forge (manually)
Where you can find it:
http://bit.ly/RoguelikeDungeons

Complexity Level: 1.5 Diamonds
Adds Items?: No
Adds Mobs?: No

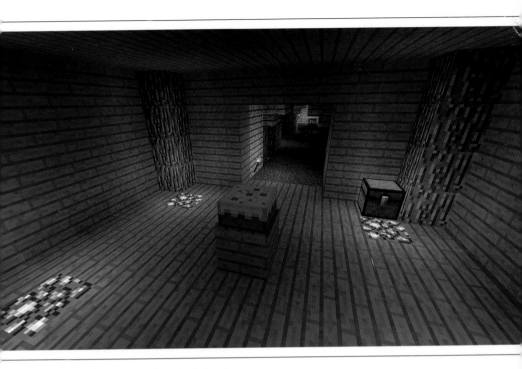

Fortresses, Abandoned Mineshafts, and regular Dungeons in Minecraft are pretty hard to find, and though they're neat, they tend to repeat themselves a lot and not be all that exciting once you've explored your first one.

Roguelike Dungeons takes the concept of randomly generated structures and kicks it up a notch, adding in dungeons that are not just gigantic, but also full of random surprises like rooms with Cake, little pre-built base-style rooms with Beds, Crafting Tables, and much more. There are even cute little decorations scattered about and a large variety in the shape of the structures, all of which combines to make for a really fun addition to vanilla Minecraft. Of course, these things are also chock full of mob spawners too, so you'll have to fight your way through one to get to all of its goodies and cool rooms.

Camping Mod

Creator: Rikmuld

In one sentence: Make every night out in the wilderness a classic adventure with camping gear and a new campfire cooking system!

Version: 1.4.7, 1.5.1, 1.5.2, 1.6.2, 1.6.4, 1.7.10
Installed Through: Forge (manually)
Where you can find it:
http://bit.ly/CampingModLink

Complexity Level: 1.5 Diamonds
Adds Items?: Yes
Adds Mobs?: Yes

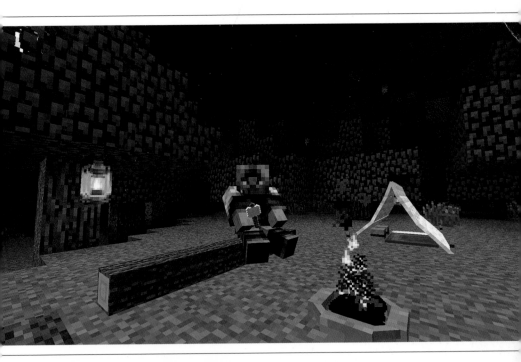

Some of the mods in this chapter add an entire new world to adventure in, while others, like this Camping Mod, are there to make your adventures feel more complete and rich. This mod is one of our favorites for just that reason, as it adds in the fun and comfort of camping and campfires to vanilla Minecraft.

This mod is very well-realized, as it contains not just new items like a Pan, Tents, Sleeping Bags and logs to sit on, it also adds a cooking system through a special Cooking Campfire, and even a couple new wild mobs (Bear and Arctic Fox)! You can even roast marshmallows, which is just a great touch.

Your nights out in the world on your exploration trips will never be dark and dreary again, with this adorable and fun little mod.

Ascension

Creator: TheXFactor117

In one sentence: Originally based on Skyrim, this mod is meant to add a fantasy adventure to your game, complete with monsters to fight, weapons to find and use, a bunch of new buildings that will randomly spawn, and a big overall quest to follow.

Version: 1.7.10
Installed Through: Forge (manually)
Where you can find it:
http://bit.ly/MinecraftAscension

Complexity Level: 3.5 Diamonds
Adds Items?: Yes
Adds Mobs?: Yes

Ascension creator TheXFactor117 makes this caveat on his mod's forum page: "This mod is meant to be challenging. I wouldn't be surprised if you died the moment you spawn — unfortunately, that's how it is. I'm here to tell you not to get discouraged because you can put your enemies to death with an arsenal of weaponry."

That should tell you a bit about Ascension, which is meant to add a quite challenging fantasy aspect and quest to vanilla Minecraft. This is one of those bigger mods that you'll notice right away (hence the warning that you might die in the previous quote), mostly because of its mobs and new structures. Once you've mastered just staying alive in Ascension, you've also got an extensive quest to find five ancient artifacts to go on, which involves fighting a boss mod, The Pharaoh!

This mod is also set to get a very big update soon, and it is one that is managed with passion and care by its creators, which makes it a great one to invest time in.

Orespawn

Creator: TheyCallMeDanger, MeganLorraine, and the Orespawn team

In one sentence: Orespawn is a polished honker of a mod that adds a ton of everything to Minecraft, including mobs, items, blocks, systems, biomes, dimensions, new things to do, and really just too much to list.

Version: 1.6.4, 1.7.10
Installed Through: Forge (manually)
Where you can find it:
http://www.orespawn.com/

Complexity Level: 5 Diamonds
Adds Items?: Yes
Adds Mobs?: Yes

Adventure Enhancers

One of our biggest modpacks in the book, Orespawn is a comprehensive total overhaul of the game in just about every way. It contains mods with focuses on armor and weapons, tons of new mobs and bosses, at least half a dozen new dimensions to travel to, gardening, building, dozens of new plants and trees and even, oddly enough, the ability to get a girlfriend in the game.

The best way to really get a feel for what Orespawn can do to transform your game (and it will transform it, inside and out) is to play it, but the second best would be to take a look at the list of "Things to Do" Orespawn lists in its guides on its website. Here's a little excerpt of some of the most interesting and oddest entries on that list, to whet your appetite to play this most excellent mod:

- **Fight Mobzilla.** Or just watch him as he destroys the entire Village Dimension...

- **Ride a Hoverboard!**

- **Build yourself a home in the Crystal Dimension.** Stay awake and watch the chaos!

- **BUILD A ZOO!!!!!** Don't forget to use the ZooKeeper Items on your critters!

- **Plant a garden** with moth plants and some torches in the Utopia Dimension. Kick your feet up and relax a bit.

- **Make a dance floor** under an Experience tree and stay up late dancing with your Girlfriend.

- **Defeat a few of the major mobs:** Water Dragon, Basilisc, Emperor Scorpion, Alien's little brother, Robo-Warrior, Kyuubi...

- **Ride a Cephadrome at night,** really slow, really low. It's like riding a mob-mower!

- **Find a Basilisc maze,** and get through it without cheating.

- **Make a bag of Popcorn.**

- **Make a Corn Dog!**

- **Mine some rubies and make yourself a Thunderstaff!**

- **Ride a Giant Spider Robot!!!!!**

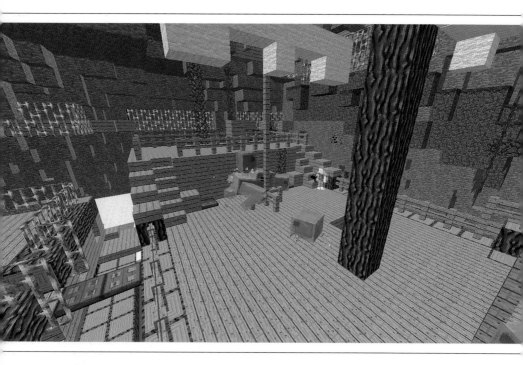

Chocolate Quest

Creator: Chocolatin, Arlo the Epic, and the
Chocolate Quest team

In one sentence: Another large adventure-
focused overhaul to the game, Chocolate
Quest adds in armor and weapons, mobs,
dungeons of many kinds, bosses, many new
pieces of equipment and tools, and even
some funky stuff like mechs!

Version: 1.5.2, 1.6.4, 1.7.2, 1.7.10
Installed Through: Forge (manually)
Where you can find it:
http://bit.ly/ChocolateQuest

Complexity Level: 4 Diamonds
Adds Items?: Yes
Adds Mobs?: Yes

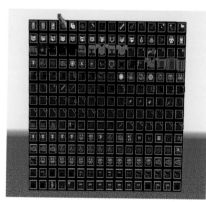

Though perhaps not quite as massive of a modpack as Orespawn or FTB Infinity, Chocolate Quest is up there with the big boys in terms of the amount of things it changes and adds to the game.

This mod was once called Better Dungeons, and though it has expanded beyond that simple, great concept by quite a bit, that title does give you a bit of an idea on what Chocolate Quest is about and how it's different from other big modpacks. Most of Chocolate Quest's items, mobs, and new blocks come from or are involved in the new dungeons it adds to the game, of which there are six different types.

DUNGEONS ADDED BY CHOCOLATE CRAFT:

Castles: These come in two types: randomly generated structures (each looks unique), and a set of pre-made "schematic" castles that have been specially designed. Each has a specific type of armed mob guarding its treasures as well as a boss.

Nether Cities: These are kind-of like bigger, more complex Villages, but for Pigmen and built over Lava. There are a large number of possible structures that can spawn, and there are new versions of the Pigmen that are much more dangerous.

NPC Villages: Majorly overhauled versions of regular Villages, with new buildings and the ability to interact with Villagers much more extensively. You can even take quests from them!

Pirate Ships: Found on the sea, not surprisingly, these can take the form of boats or the dread pirate island, and they are all covered in bloodthirsty pirates of many kinds that want nothing more than to cut you up a bit.

Snow Castles: Only in the Tundra biome will you find these mighty fortresses, which house the Abyss Walkers and a ton of traps. The makers of Chocolate Quest warn the player that these are some of the most difficult dungeons to clear in an already difficult mod, but the rewards are said to be great.

Player-Made Dungeons: A very cool feature of this mod is that you can import dungeons into it that other players, or you yourself, have made! There's a list and instructions available at the Chocolate Quest website, so once you've had your fill of the regular dungeons, there's plenty more to check out!

TerrafirmaCraft

Creator: Bioxx, Dunkleosteus, Kittychanley, and the TerrafirmaCraft team

In one sentence: Takes every step of crafting and surviving in vanilla Minecraft and makes it much more difficult, more complicated and more rewarding, as it adds major numbers of new items and systems to learn.

Version: 1.7.10
Installed Through: Forge (manually)
Where you can find it:
http://terrafirmacraft.com

Complexity Level: 5 Diamonds
Adds Items?: Yes
Adds Mobs?: Yes

TerrafirmaCraft is a mod that is very often included in modpacks for its high quality of upgraded vanilla play. By upgraded vanilla, we mean that this mod is very true to regular vanilla Minecraft's feel and style, it just takes it and adds in a whole lot more items and steps.

For instance, getting tools in the early game is no longer as easy as going straight from Wood tools to Stone. First you have to build a basic tool by smashing rocks together in a realistic "knapping" system, and you can't even punch a tree to get Wood anymore!

Realism is the name of the game with TerrafirmaCraft, whose tagline is "Survival mode as it should have been." The idea is that Minecraft's regular survival mode, fun as it is, is also not one bit realistic with all of the tree punching and ability to very quickly create advanced tools and items. In TerrafirmaCraft, you'll find that you have to go through very logical and complete steps to do even something as simple as making your first Pickaxe, which will require that you build each piece of the axe and use a special type of table to get a design for a Pickaxe made.

The result of the new systems in this mod is an undoubtedly harder survival experience, where each new thing you're able to build is difficult but immensely rewarding to complete. To some that will seem too stressful, but for those of us who love the feeling of just barely scraping by on your wits and ingenuity, this is the premier mod to play.

Atum

Creator: Shadowclaimer and Lclc98

In one sentence: Throws a new dimension into Minecraft with an ancient Egyptian-style feel and new items, mobs, and awesome dungeons to explore.

Version: 1.5, 1.6.4, 1.7.10
Installed Through: Forge (manually)
Where you can find it:
http://bit.ly/AtumMod

Complexity Level: 3.5 Diamonds
Adds Items?: Yes
Adds Mobs?: Yes

A lighter adventure enhancing mod, Atum is still pretty complex. It would also fit decently well in our biomes chapter, but because the desert dimension it creates has much the same look and feel as the vanilla desert, we've put it here. This is also because Atum's focus is on giving you a new place to adventure in, with mobs to slay and treasure to acquire.

This treasure, which comes in the form of many new items, is one of the major draws for Atum, as it has one of the best and most creative item set designs in any mod. The weapons and armor, for instance, have an incredibly lavish, bejeweled appearance, and decking yourself out in a full set just looks plain cool.

You'll often see this mod in packs, partly because of this mod's aesthetic, and also for the fun of its many randomly spawned dungeons. There are a variety of these, each with its own unique design and potentially a boss, but the most fun we had was exploring the very well-done, complex and trap-filled maze that took up the inside of the massive pyramids. If you can survive to reach the top, your troubles have just begun!

Shape Shifter

Creator: zacuke

In one sentence: Become every mob in the game, complete with special powers for each mob.

Version: 1.6.4
Installed Through: Forge (manually)
Where you can find it:
http://bit.ly/ShapeShifterMod

Complexity Level: 2 Diamonds
Adds Items?: No
Adds Mobs?: No, but tweaks them

This mod doesn't change the look of the game really at all, and it could be considered on the smaller and less complex end of the spectrums, but it is a bit of a game changer. That's because the shape shifting ability it gives you, which lets you become any mob in the game, really changes the way you move about and interact with the world of Minecraft.

That's not hard to imagine, when you think about what you'd do in vanilla Minecraft if you could suddenly become an Ender Dragon and fly around. Each mob has an ability or two like this, and it makes for a very different experience without changing what the rest of the game is like. It's even more pronounced on multiplayer, and we highly suggest getting a bunch of your friends around and Squid-ing about the ocean just for fun.

Most popular mobs to turn into, data gathered by zacuke:

1. Dragon
2. Ocelot
3. Bat
4. Creeper
5. Enderman
6. Spider
7. Villager
8. Zombie
9. Ghast
10. Wither
11. Wolf
12. Silverfish
13. Sheep
14. Chicken
15. Slime
16. Pig
17. Golem
18. Skeleton
19. Blaze
20. Squid
21. Magmacube
22. Witch
23. Snowman
24. Cow
25. Mooshroom
??. Horse

FloorBallCraft

Creator: TheLarsinator

In one sentence: Adds everything you need to play a game similar to hockey or lacrosse in Minecraft.

Version: 1.6.4, 1.7.2, 1.7.10
Installed Through: Forge (manually)
Where you can find it:
http://bit.ly/FloorBallCraft

Complexity Level: 2 Diamonds
Adds Items?: Yes
Adds Mobs?: No

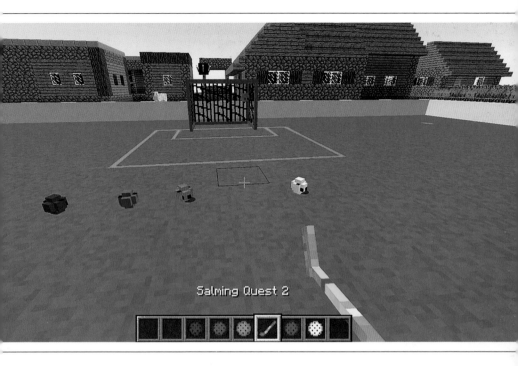

Salming Quest 2

We're using the term "adventure" a bit loosely here, but hey, stopping to play a highly competitive game in the middle of nowhere against your rivals can totally be a part of an adventure, right? We think it just adds another layer of fun and more memories to the game, and that's why we've put the fun and lightweight FloorBallCraft in this chapter.

FloorBallCraft has two options: you can either use the items that come with it to build your own court on which to play, including even painting the lines down and crafting a Goal piece-by-piece, or you can just download a pre-made rink and get to playin'! The game itself is, as mentioned, much the same as hockey or lacrosse where you're just trying to use a stick to get a ball in a net, and it works pretty well for a game built inside of another game. Well worth a try, and hey, maybe you could even get a league going if you get enough friends!

LotsOMobs

Creator: TheLarsinator

In one sentence: Primarily a large-scale mob adder, but this mod goes in the adventure chapter because it also adds dimensions, items, crops systems, and blocks.

Version: 1.6.2, 1.6.4, 1.7.2, 1.7.10, 1.8
Installed Through: Forge (manually)
Where you can find it:
http://bit.ly/LotsOMobsMod

Complexity Level: 3.5 Diamonds
Adds Items?: Yes
Adds Mobs?: Yes

Adventure Enhancers

Made by the same guy that did FloorBallCraft, LotsOMobs is a more traditional Minecraft adventure enhancing mod. You might think from the name and the fact that it includes more than 45 new mobs that it would go in our mobs chapter, but this mod goes far beyond its namesake and adds in many other features to kick your adventure into another gear.

Maybe the most awesome additions are the new dimensions LotsOMobs adds in, which include an Ice Age and a Dinosaur Dimension. Guess what you'll find in that last one? Yep, a whole lot of dinos, all ready to stomp you flat and eat your little Crafter body.

There are also new tools, crops, weapons, blocks, and more in this mod, as well as new tanning and DNA systems that allow you to create some of the items and even mobs added by LotsOMobs. TheLarsinator is a very good modder with a lot of interesting stuff to offer the community, and LotsOMobs may be his best work. It's certainly worth a go for the Dino Dimension alone.

Magic, Tech, And Crafting Systems
Beyond Redstone And Basic Crafting

If Redstone is the hardest, most complex part of Minecraft to get a handle on, think of the mods in this chapter as the Redstone of this book. They are all systems of items that interact with each other in various ways, some not so complex and some that make Redstone itself look like the first day of kindergarten.

This is the section for those who want to make the world of Minecraft do more. That is, make resources matter more and have more options, have more goals of items to build and systems to create, to automate more, or to become more powerful as a character. All of that and more is here, where we're talking Minecraft systems, from magic to tech to those that do both to those that do something else entirely.

It should be noted that these are, except for the modpacks (many of which include quite a few of these mods), the most difficult to master and dense mods in the book. Some of these will walk you through how to use them as you go, but most won't, and we can't recommend enough that you go online to learn more about each mod. Not only will there be things like wikis that, for some mods, are almost as long as this entire book, but you'll also find thousands of people in the forums and other places learning the mod right alongside you. These are invaluable resources, and everyone starting out on one of these awesome magic, tech, and crafting systems mods should use them.

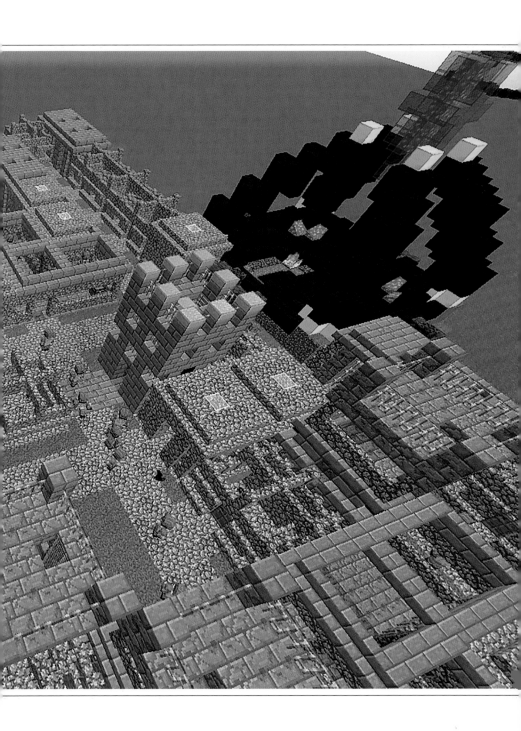

Railcraft

In one sentence: Real trains and much better track systems added on to the regular Minecraft Rails system.

Version: 1.5.2, 1.6.2, 1.6.4, 1.7.2, 1.7.10
Installed Through: Forge (manually)
Where you can find it:
bit.ly/RailCraftMod

Complexity Level: 3 Diamonds
Adds Items?: Yes
Adds Mobs?: No

The Rails system in Minecraft is actually pretty primitive when compared to even the most basic real-world train track, and the popular Railcraft mod sets that wrong right, and then some. It adds all manner of new tracks and cart items, as well as fixing some pesky issues with Minecarts, such as making the physics more realistic. It sounds simple, but the things you can do with Railcraft get quite complex and can lead to some really amazing automated builds, as well as doing some fun things like giving you a new way to dig cool looking tunnels for trains and giving you a "Launch Track," which does just what it sounds like it would.

Dynamic Glass

Mekanism

Creator: aidancbrady

In one sentence: A highly complex tech mod, with multiple tech tiers and systems like ore processing and salinaton to learn.

Version: 1.7.10
Installed Through: Forge (manually), also has submods that can be included if wanted
Where you can find it:
http://aidancbrady.com/

Complexity Level: 4 Diamonds
Adds Items?: Oh yes
Adds Mobs?: No

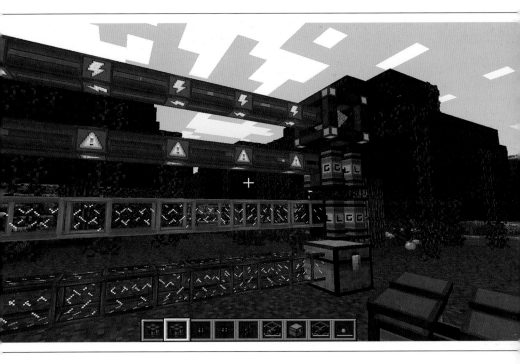

Here's a tidbit from Mekanism's website to get you enticed to download what is certainly one of Minecraft's premier tech mods: "By the time you've been using Mekanism for a while, you'll have a near-instructible suit of Obsidian Armor, be obtaining four ingots for each ore you mine, have the ability to fly wherever you want with the hydrogen-powered jetpacks, and have a cute robotic friend following you around while you mine."

That's a heck of a mod pitch, and creator Aidan C Brady's mod more than lives up to it. Brady is, like many of the creators in this book, not even in college yet, and he's already created what is one of the most respected high-tech mods in the game. In just the last update alone Aidan has added Flamethrowers, Lasers, new resources, Baby Skeletons (adorable!), the intense-sounding Solar Neutron Activator, and the, as he puts it, "ultimate end-game energy production" system of Fusion Reactors.

Mekanism is killer, and Brady seems set on making coding a career. As part of his portfolio, expect Mekanism to continue to receive updates and support for a good while, and expect it all to be of the highest quality.

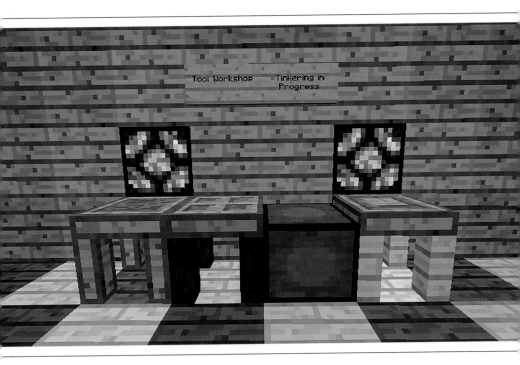

Tinkers' Construct

Creator: mDiyo, boni, and Jadedcat

In one sentence: Greatly expands tool-making, adding many new tables that are involved in different ways, such as making parts for tools, adding modifiers to them or repairing them.

Version: 1.6.4, 1.7.10
Installed Through: Forge (manually)
Where you can find it:
http://bit.ly/TinkersConstructMod

Complexity Level: 4 Diamonds
Adds Items?: Yes
Adds Mobs?: Yes

Tinkers' Construct takes the regular method of crafting tools and items through a Crafting Table and makes it much more powerful, adding multiple types of crafting stations, tables, and forges. Players use Patterns to build each individual part of the tool they want. There are also new types of tools to be made, like Rapiers, Chisels, and Frying Pans, and you now have to take many steps to create them, like using patterns to make the parts of each tool.

This makes for a much richer tool-creating experience, and it also makes things better in the long run by making tool modifiers available (and not just through regular Enchanting Tables), as well as making tools repairable, so you never have to lose them (saves resources and time!).

Tinkers' Construct also has an extensive armor creation system for special, very high-quality armor, and it adds in a new system for turning metals into liquid, which is needed for some of its tool creation.

ICBM Mod

Creator: Robert Seifert, Calclavia, and dmodoomsirius

In one sentence: Missiles in Minecraft.

Version: 1.6.4, 1.7.10
Installed Through: Forge (manually)
Where you can find it:
http://bit.ly/ICBMModLink

Complexity Level: 3 Diamonds
Adds Items?: Yes
Adds Mobs?: No

TNT cannons are one of the genius creations in Minecraft that the community created all on its own, without Mojang really designing TNT with that in mind. However, they are clunky, not all that powerful and not always predictable.

ICBM mod is launched explosives brought to Minecraft in a full, well-designed way. It contains many, many kinds of missiles based on real-world weapons, but the massive destruction they bring on the heads of your enemies is all virtual, meaning you can finally blow the crap out of your enemies with massive missiles and not feel bad about it at all (or, y'know, have to become a military leader).

As the documentation on the mod points out, this mod is especially interesting when paired with something like a Factions server online where blowing up bases is a major part of play. Having real missiles to work with and not janky TNT cannons makes for an entirely new experience, and one which is sure to get quite explosive in more than one way.

Magic Items Mod

Creator: SimJoo

In one sentence: Essentially gives players a huge number of magic powers based on various craftable items including flight, taking no damage, invisibility, teleportation, speed, explosions, and a ton more.

Version: 1.7.2, 1.7.10
Installed Through: Forge (manually)
Where you can find it:
http://bit.ly/MagicItems

Complexity Level: 3.5 Diamonds
Adds Items?: Yes
Adds Mobs?: No

The background story on Magic Items, according to its PMC page, goes like this: "About 2 months ago me and my friends started running a Forge server. We've searched all the minecraft mods, but couldn't find a mod that was compatible with every other mod and that added a lot of stuff to mess around with. That's why I made this mod. This mod is compatible with every mod on earth and adds a load of items to mess around with and that are great for use in survival."

That last bit about a load of items is no joke. Magic Items Mod has so many, well, magic items that it would normally go in our Items chapter, but because those items interact with and add an extensive system of magic, we've put it here. Where many magic mods are based around spells or other sorts of systems that use items but have other aspects, Magic Items is simpler in its approach. All magic that can be done through it happens simply by crafting and using these items, of which there are many.

Among the things that Magic Items' magic items will let you do are teleporting to different dimensions, flying about on magic clouds, breathing underwater, and even some weird stuff, like faking that a player is hurting you, shaking your head, and causing particles or sounds to happen when their corresponding event or mob isn't around (maybe all at once, in some sort of elaborate prank).

Additionally there are some new, highly powerful weapons and tools from Magic Items and, maybe most useful, a way to build elevators that works much better than regular Redstone elevators (which often barely work at all).

JABBA

Creator: ProfMobius and Taelnia

In one sentence: As the name says, it's Just Another Better Barrel Attempt which makes a new way to store things that is much quicker, easier, and barrel-inclusive.

Version: 1.6.4, 1.7.2, 1.7.10
Installed Through: Forge (manually)
Where you can find it:
http://bit.ly/JABBAMod

Complexity Level: 2.5 Diamonds
Adds Items?: Yes
Adds Mobs?: No

ProfMobius is a veteran and leader in the mod scene, putting in work on a few other mods in this book (DecoCraft and Waila, to name just two) and getting his excellent mods included in many modpacks. Among those, JABBA, or Just Another Better Barrel Attempt, is one of the most common to find in packs and on servers.

This is because JABBA makes storage a breeze by adding in the Barrel. Instead of having to open the Barrel like you would a Chest, Barrels can be interacted with and filled or depleted using various types of clicks. For instance, right-clicking the Barrel with an item stack will place it in it, while left-clicking will remove a stack, and double right-clicking will put all items of that kind in the Barrel. Barrels also can take input from any direction, which means they have many uses with automated systems.

While not a massive new tech system, these Better Barrels are an example of a small problem being fixed by a mod that makes that mod highly useful when combined with others, something that is important to things like modpacks or finding a selection of mods to use on your own server.

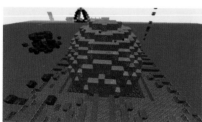

Blood Magic

Creator: WayofTime

In one sentence: A dark, full-featured magic system that features everything from sacrificial rituals to dangerous potion brewing and sigil creation.

Version: 1.6.4, 1.7.2, 1.7.10
Installed Through: Forge (manually)
Where you can find it:
http://bit.ly/BloodMagicLink

Complexity Level: 4 Diamonds
Adds Items?: Yes
Adds Mobs?: Yes

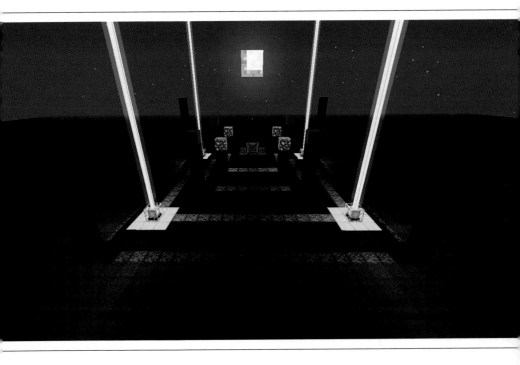

We love when a mod goes all in on its background and aesthetic, and when it comes to magic systems, Blood Magic does this better than any other. It also eschews the idea that Minecraft's world needs to be a cute and cuddly one in favor of bringing a bit of darkness and blood to the game, which is a whole dang lot of fun.

We talked to creator WayofTime about his mod, and he gave us this excellent description:

"Blood Magic: possibly one of the most arcane of all arts, this branch of magic can either utilize the life essence of the willing or the blood of the forced. One of the key aspects that is present throughout the mod is weighing the attainment of ultimate power with the costs that can come with such a morally ambiguous path. There are several paths that the player may go down, such as building intricate in-world spells, to brewing complex potions and poisons with alchemy, to even building a giant altar to either sacrifice your foes or your own life force. There is no sight quite like building a complicated ritual under the open sky and summoning forth a meteor full of riches!

The path is a long one, full of challenges that will push you towards greater power. Several branches of magic all collapsing into one source of power that comes from the life force of others. The real question that you have to ask yourself is this: what is your limit when it comes to attaining the power of a demon?"

Applied Energistics 2

Creator: AlgorithmX2, Cisien, thatsIch, fireball1725, akarso, and the Applied Energistics team

In one sentence: The ultimate engineering mod, with so many crafting, item transportation and manipulation systems that you'll never get bored (if that's your thing).

Version: 1.7.10
Installed Through: Forge (manually)
Where you can find it:
http://ae-mod.info/

Complexity Level: 4.5 Diamonds
Adds Items?: Yes
Adds Mobs?: No

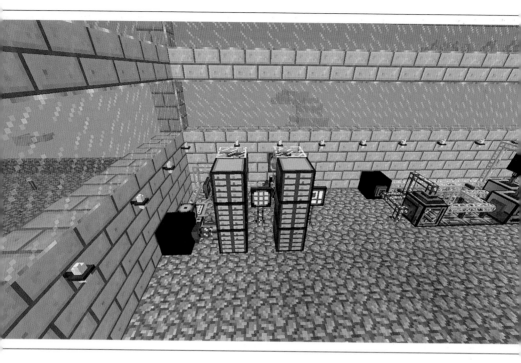

This is a very complex one. Essentially, Applied Energistics 2 is a very physics/reality based engineering system for Minecraft that makes basic Redstone look quite easy. The core concepts are based around, according to the mod's homepage, "the concept of using Energy, and the Transformation of Energy in a unique way."

Bytes, MegaJoules, and other real-world measuring systems become a part of Minecraft through Applied Energistics, and most of the mod is based around the creation of complex integrated systems called Matter Energy Networks. These networks can perform an absolutely mind-bending number of functions, most especially those related to automation and item transportation.

For those who want to build wild, enormous factories with the best, most complex and efficient automation possible, you need to give Applied Energistics a try. It's also perfect for those who want a serious challenge akin to learning Redstone, but much more complex.

Pam's Mods

Creator: Pam, aka MatrexsVigil

In one sentence: Turns farming and planting into much more complex systems, with many, many more plants and items to use as well as new recipes.

Version: Either up to 1.7.10 or 1.7.2, depending on the mod
Installed Through: Forge (manually)
Where you can find it:
http://bit.ly/PamsModsLink

Complexity Level: 3 Diamonds (overall)
Adds Items?: Yes
Adds Mobs?: Sort-of, adds more Fish and also Bees

This is a mod for nature lovers and those who want to extensively amplify the way they interact with plants and natural blocks (different types of dirts and stones etc.) in Minecraft. We include it in the systems chapter because it adds so very many different recipes and new items to use to craft them that it is more than just a mod with an incredible number of new, great items. Just wander around a world with Pam's Mods loaded and you'll see the difference immediately, with ever so much more color being added due to all the new crops and plants like Apples, Pears, Lemons, Coconuts and more in trees; Beans, Ginger, Tea, and Cucumbers in the ground; and ever so much more.

Pam's mods are truly a horticulturist's dream, as well as a mineralogist's, as Pam has also included new types of ores and other natural blocks in her mods. Though these don't come as one pack, they're all so well-done, compatible and easy to install in your world that we've included Pam's whole run of mods in our entry here. Just about every world will benefit from Pam's mods, and all we have to do to prove it is to tell you that you can craft Fried Pickles and a Bacon Cheeseburger with just Harvestcraft (by Pam) alone.

Extended Farming

Creator: TheLarsinator

In one sentence: Makes farming much more realistic and efficient with systems like irrigation, tractors and even Lava pumping (plus new crops and a new mob).

Version: 1.7.10
Installed Through: Forge (manually)
Where you can find it:
http://bit.ly/ExtendedFarming

Complexity Level: 3.5 Diamonds
Adds Items?: Yes
Adds Mobs?: Yes

Pam's Mods are mostly about adding items in and a few new systems, and they actually work great with our mod here by TheLarsinator, which is primarily focused on the actual farming part of food production.

Never again will you have to go through and pick plants by hand like it's ancient times, or use actual streams of Water to keep things growing; Extended Farming adds in tractors and irrigation systems just like they are used in real-world farming. On top of that, you get the fun of a few new crops to use these tools on, and even the quirky Goat mob to farm and friend.

TheLarsinator has plans to keep this one growing, with spices, fertilizers, greenhouses, and many more mobs and crops said to be on the way.

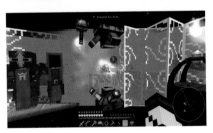

Thaumcraft

Creator: Azanor

In one sentence: An extensive magic systems mod based around the idea of taking power from natural objects using Wands and many other systems.

Version: 1.7.10 and back
Installed Through: Forge (manually)
Where you can find it:
http://bit.ly/ThaumcraftModLink

Complexity Level: 4 Diamonds
Adds Items?: Yes
Adds Mobs?: Yes

If mods like Applied Energistics are the highly complex mods of the engineering and tech worlds, Thaumcraft is the same for magic. The progression trees for building and manipulating items like Wands and more in Thaumcraft, in order to get more magic a'goin' in your world, are highly complex and in depth, with an absolutely staggering amount to do.

Just in terms of magic, you've got not only Thaumaturgy ("the working of miracles"), which is mostly Wand-based, you'll also be messing about with the powers of alchemy, artifice, golemancy and enchanting. Each of these has a lot to it and will require exploration, mining, combat and pretty much everything else in Minecraft to master.

In support of these magic systems are a bunch of new ores, mobs, biomes, structures and pretty much everything in Minecraft, making this a thoroughly comprehensive Big Mod. All of this stuff is pretty hard to get a grasp on, but luckily the mod comes with an interactive Thaumonomicon (a book) to teach you and guide you through the whole magical shebang. All in all, it's pretty...magical (don't hate us for bad jokes).

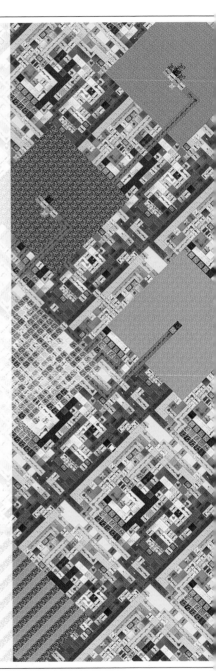

Visual
Mods
Making Minecraft Prettier

Part of Minecraft's charm is it's pixely look. It's distinctive and much of what makes Minecraft what it is, but that does not mean there is no room for improvement. The blocky, pixel-by-pixel nature of Minecraft can still be had while improving its overall graphics and/or looks greatly, whether that means something like taking its basic animations and making them smooth and dynamic, or something such as massively overhauling the way it deals with lights and shadows.

Visual mods are often what draw people to Minecraft modding in the first place. Many people see images of Minecraft builds online that just look incredibly cool, and it's obvious that they aren't made in typical Minecraft. Nine times out of ten, that's because they used one or more visual mods to change Minecraft's basic pixel look into something beautiful (or in the case of Mineshot, to actually take that beautiful image), and getting your Minecraft looking as cool as it can is what this chapter is all about.

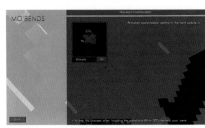

Mo'Bends

Creator: Gobbob

In one sentence: Takes the basic Minecraft movement animations and replaces them with much smoother, cool-looking animations!

Version: 1.7.2, 1.7.10
Installed Through: Forge (manually)
Where you can find it:
http://bit.ly/MoBendsLink

Complexity Level: 1 Diamond

Minecraft's regular animations are kinda cute in their simplicity, but they definitely aren't cool-lookin'. Mo'Bends changes that! The game acts exactly the same, but now every motion by you and other characters works more like animations do in more standard video games. That means Sword swings look like you're a knight and not a toddler wailing on something with a plastic hammer, and monsters attack and move much more like their counterparts in films (the Zombie hunch is pretty great!).

OptiFine

Creator: sp614x

In one sentence: An absolute Top 5 mod that takes all things visual and amps them way up while making other visual mods possible and everything run a lot faster and better while giving an intense level of customization to the way things look.

Version: Pretty much any, ever. They're very good at keeping it up to date.
Installed Through: Forge (manually)
Where you can find it:
https://optifine.net/

Complexity Level: 2 Diamonds

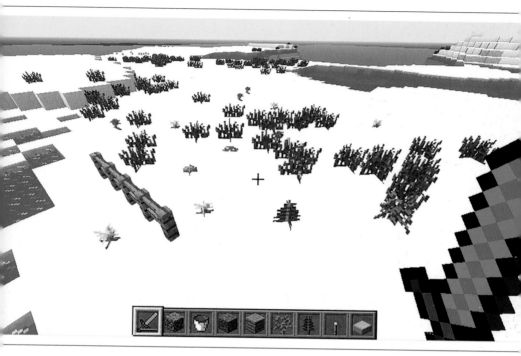

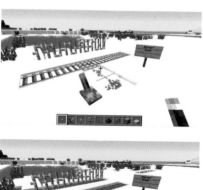

Right, so you want this one. It is a must get, if any mod in here is. When writing this book and most of the other Minecraft books we have created, we have used this one through almost the entire process.

That's because it's a genius-level creation when it comes to the visuals of Minecraft. If you've ever seen a cool picture of Minecraft, chances are they were running OptiFine, because it allows most other cool looking mods to work. Instead of writing it out in sentences, the best way to explain OptiFine is simply to list everything awesome that this thing does.

Video Settings

Graphics: Fast	Render Distance: Far +80
Smooth Lighting: OFF	Performance: Max FPS
3D Anaglyph: OFF	View Bobbing: OFF
GUI Scale: Auto	Advanced OpenGL: OFF
Brightness: +32%	Clouds: ON
Fog: Fast	Fog Start: 0.8
Details...	Quality...
Animations...	Performance...
Texture Packs...	Other...

Done

COOL THINGS OPTIFINE DOES:

- Amplifies FPS by massive amounts while making gameplay smoother at the same time

- Makes HD textures from texture packs work

- Allows the render distance to be MUCH farther than vanilla Minecraft (far more than double, though you need a good computer to run it at high distances)

- Smoothes lighting

- Smoothes textures at distances

- Causes Snow and Grass to render on blocks under things like Redstone and Fences, where it didn't before and should

- Makes Water clear! You can actually see what's under it, even when underwater

COOL THINGS OPTIFINE DOES:

· Flips nature textures around so that they don't just repeat in a grid

· Connects other textures, like Glass, eliminating the lines between connected pieces

· Has better anisotropic filtering, antialiasing and mipmaps, all of which basically means it looks better overall

· Makes Autosaves customizable

· Can switch texture packs without exiting

· Makes just about everything visual customizable!

· Dang that's a lot of stuff

Mineshot

Creator: BarracudaATA

In one sentence: Creates the highest resolution, most interesting Minecraft screenshots that can be taken from inside the game.

Version: 1.7.10
Installed Through: Forge (manually)
Where you can find it:
http://bit.ly/MineshotMod

Complexity Level: 1.5 Diamonds

Visual Mods

At one point back in the early days of Minecraft, there was an official option to take very high-resolution screenshots of your game. These days that is not possible without a mod, and by far the best mod for the job is Mineshot.

Mineshot uses special keybinds to allow the player to go into a photo-taking mode that not only takes screenshots at an incredibly high resolution, it also lets you frame the shot in ways that normal Minecraft doesn't. Usually Minecraft is always from a first-person perspective, which means that the image you see is similar to one seen through a lens pointing the same direction. This means that it's curved from the center out. Mineshot can take hi-res shots from that standard perspective, but it also allows you to go from a perspective that looks at the world in front of it on a flat plane, without the curve (see screenshots).

The results of Mineshot screens are terribly impressive, and immediately recognized by other players as something special. This is another tool that pros use to take those screens that you see on websites that look like a whole different game, and what's great is that it is one of the easiest and most compatible mods to use that you can find. It works with just about any other mod that is out for the same version, and the only drag on your computer will be entirely from shaders and other mods you have running, and not Mineshot itself.

Better Foliage

Creator: OctarineNoise

In one sentence: Amplifies the looks of plants in Minecraft to a more natural, interesting representation.

Version: 1.7.10, 1.8
Installed Through: Forge (manually)
Where you can find it:
http://bit.ly/BetterFoliageMod

Complexity Level: 1 Diamond

This is a pretty simple mod, but it does make a marked difference since there are just so darn many plants in Minecraft. Essentially it takes your regular old leaves and plant materials and gives them a more realistic look, including a little bit of animation, such as for falling leaves and the like. This is another that isn't a massive change, but a subtly powerful one that changes the overall look of the game to be just that much better.

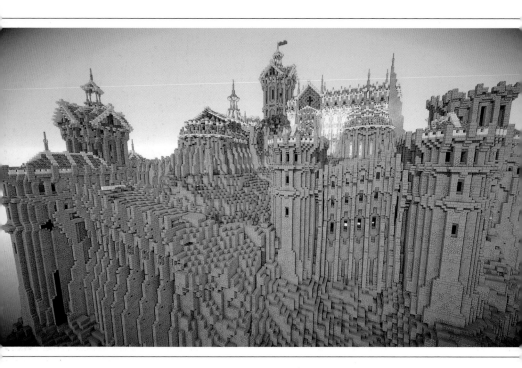

The Shader Mods

In one sentence: Take the lighting and visual representation of regular Minecraft and turn it into something dynamic, beautiful, varied, and downright gorgeous.

Installed Through: Forge (manually), requires the Shaders Mod
Shaders Mod Download:
http://bit.ly/ShadersModDownloadLink

Complexity Level: 1.5 Diamonds

Visual Mods

Shaders make Minecraft look great. Shaders are what make other games look the way they do, with variegated lighting over different textures and shadows that look nearly real. Minecraft in its vanilla form doesn't really have these; that's partially why it's so popular, because it can be run on just about any machine and Mojang doesn't have to deal with the complexities of shading.

Being the heavily moddable game that it is, however, the fanbase has gone out and created a set of shaders that can be added to Minecraft that take the basic game and turn it into something that can only be described as beautiful. There are a decent number of these shaders out there, each of which represents the light and textures of the game in its own unique and interesting way, and which you can switch between once you've loaded them into the game's folders in the right way.

Doing this requires getting the core mod for shaders, called (unsurprisingly) the Shaders Mod. You can find this mod at the link we've listed at the start of this section, which will also show you the correct folder to load individual shaders into. All that you need to do after that is to find a few good shaders online, download them and stick them in the "Shaders" folder in the Minecraft directory on your computer, and then select them from the options menus once you've loaded up the game. You'll notice the difference immediately when you get a shader properly loaded. In fact, if you've ever seen a really cool screenshot or video of Minecraft and wondered how it looked so dang good, there's no question that it was shaders that were responsible for the prettiness.

Note: Shaders can be a bit tricky depending on the computer you're running them on, and not all shaders work on all machines. Try a few out and see what works for you, and always keep in mind that shaders, massively increase the drag on your computer's memory and processor. If you have a very high-powered computer, or if you get a lower level of shader, this shouldn't be a problem for regular gameplay, but if you have a more standard computer, shaders really aren't going to be much use except for screenshotting, as they will cause heavy lag on your game.

A short list of some good shaders and where to get them is here; for more just head to the Shaders Mod link listed previously, or Google "Minecraft Shaders."

EXCELLENT SHADERS:

Sonic Ether's Unbelievable Shaders:
http://bit.ly/ShadersSonicEthers

Sildur's Shaders:
bit.ly/SildursShadersLink

Chocapic13's Shaders:
http://bit.ly/Chocapic13ShadersLink

Mr. Meepz's Shaders:
http://bit.ly/MrMeepzShaders

Odd **Mod Spotlight**

Second Screen Mod

Creator: maxanier

In one sentence: A mod that sends information about your Minecraft world to an app on a second screen! Whoa!

Version: 1.6.4, 1.7.2, 1.7.10, 1.8
Installed Through: Forge (manually)
Where you can find it:
http://bit.ly/MinecraftSecondScreen

Complexity Level: 2 Diamonds

This weird, wonderful little mod just didn't fit anywhere else, but is too cool not to include in this book. The Second Screen Mod is a genius piece of coding that allows you to open up an app on a phone or through a website which gives you information about your Minecraft world and can even let you interact with it in a limited way. It can be used either on a second screen right next to your first, or when you're not even at home, as long as the server your game is on is up and running!

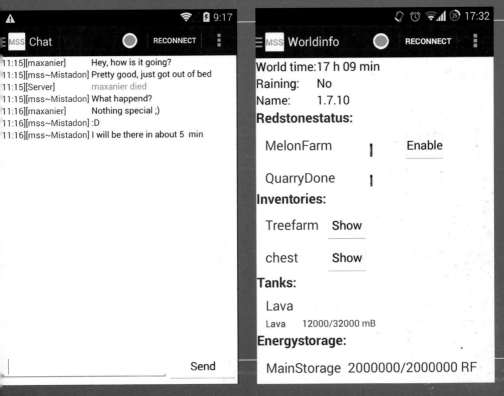

In terms of what you can actually do with it, the Second Screen Mod is pretty darn impressive. It can show you basic information such as the time of of day and weather status in your world, and it can also give you info on who's on your server, what their health is or what food level they're at.

The interactable stuff is even cooler, as you can now chat with players in-world from the app without logging into the game yourself, and you can even do things like check inventories in chests and activate or deactivate Redstone switches.

This is a very unique mod, and it's pretty much alone in doing any of these cool things it does, and it is well worth setting up on any server that you use frequently.

The
Technic **Mod**
Launcher

Of the mod loaders out there, the Technic Launcher is among the two most popular that do all the work for you (along with Feed the Beast's loader), and for good reason. Not only is it simple, cool-looking, and very stable, it also includes some of the best mods and modpacks that have yet been called into the Minecraft world. In fact, many of the most beloved mods in existence, like Galacticraft and Thaumcraft, are contained in the major Technic modpacks alongside some lesser known mods (turn yourself into a hamster!), and the result is an experience that we think might possibly be the best way to play Minecraft.

To get Technic mods going on your own system is a thoroughly simple process. Simply head to this link and get the loader: **www.technicpack.net/**

Once you've done that, you can browse through various mods on the loader itself if you're looking for their big-time mods, or you can use the Technic website to find some of the more obscure mods. Installing is as easy as pressing the install button on the loader or, for those smaller mods from the site, you can snag a mod's link and copy-paste it into the "Add Pack or Search" feature of the Technic loader's "Modpacks" tab. When it comes to loading in a large number of mods, especially when trying to get mods to work together, it doesn't come easier than the Technic loader.

A Era do Futuro

In one sentence: A major collection of popular mods with a wide scope that adds a little of everything.

Approximate Mod Count: 40+
Complexity Level: 5 Diamonds

Adds Items?: Yes
Adds Mobs?: Yes

A Era do Futuro is a highly popular modpack on the Technic system, and that's not surprising one bit: A Era contains over 40 of the Minecraft world's most beloved mods. In a nutshell, it overhauls pretty much every facet of the game, including the biomes (with mod Extra Biomes XL), the mobs (Mo'Zombies, Mutant Creatures, Primitive Mobs, and more), the weapons (Asgard Shield, Legend Gear, More Bows, and more), and just about everything else. With A Era do Futuro, you'll be able to build amazing machines, fly to space, travel through a fantasy forest dimension, and ever so much more, making it one of the best modpacks to wet your whistle with when starting out. Even the trees are amazing in this one!

Attack of the B-Team

In one sentence: Weird, wacky, wild stuff that makes Minecraft into a world where you never know what you'll be able to do or find next.

Approximate Mod Count: 70
Complexity Level: 5 Diamonds

Adds Items?: Yes
Adds Mobs?: Yes

Wacky honestly doesn't begin to describe this mod for lovers of the weird and the just plain fun. Attack of the B-Team's site says it all when it explains that it "was designed with one thing in mind, crazy mad science! With the help of the B-Team we hand picked the wackiest mods we could find and shoved them all in a modpack for you guys."

In it you'll find all the best mods that have a strange twist to them, like the Hats mod which, as you might guess, adds a ton of hats for both you and mobs, or the Morph mod, which lets you turn into other creatures such as mobs. Combine that one with the Hamsterrific and Hamsters Forever mod, the awesome giant, exploding, purple-shooting dubstep gun from the Sainstpack, and a whole lot more, and you can see how Attack of the B-Team is one of the most fun, if most bizarre, modpacks that's been made. If the fact that you can ride an Enderdragon isn't enough to get you downloading this mod, we don't know what will be.

Official Crafting Dead

In one sentence: *The Walking Dead* + Minecraft, complete with new health systems, guns and, if you hadn't guessed it yet, a ton of Zombies.

Complexity Level: 3.5 Diamonds

Adds Items?: Yes
Adds Mobs?: Sort-of, tweaks Zombies

Official Crafting Dead is, as the name might give you a slight hint about, a Minecraft mod based loosely on everyone's favorite zombie apocalypse TV show, *The Walking Dead*. As the creators say, it's also got a little DayZ thrown in there, and with the popularity of both that game and the show, there's no better time to jump into Official Crafting Dead.

And don't expect this to just be Minecraft + a crapload of zombies; it is that (of course), but Official Crafting Dead also throws in a whole new set of survival and combat-related features such as a ton of new weapons (guns!), new biomes, and systems that tell you whether you're being too loud, too visible, or are getting too thirsty. The new user interface for Crafting Dead shows you everything from your kill count, to how loud you're being, to even how much blood you have left (don't let that last one hit zero, by the way), making for much more intense combat, and you can even fall and break your legs, which is weirdly awesome.

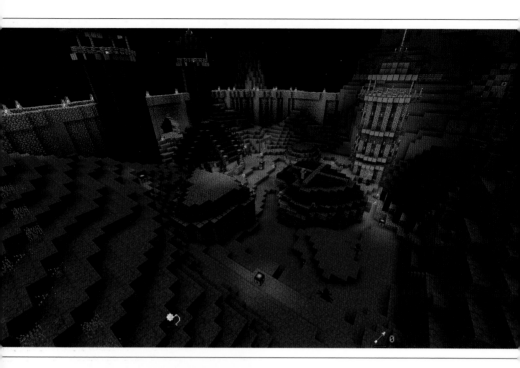

Hexxit

In one sentence: The ultimate fantasy modpack that isn't set in the world of an existing franchise (like The Fellowship is), turning vanilla Minecraft into a magical high adventure.

Approximate Mod Count: 50+
Complexity Level: 5 Diamonds

Adds Items?: Yes
Adds Mobs?: Yes

Like wizards and spells and trolls and all that wonderful fantasy stuff? Then you'll love Hexxit, the premier magic-based modpack and another excellent addition to the Technic Launcher. Similar to The Fellowship, but with the idea that you're creating your own adventure in a world no one's ever seen but you (as opposed to the world of Middle Earth).

Hexxit really changes the way you play Minecraft,
not only because you're able to cast spells, build new weapons and fight all sorts of mythical and mystical new mobs, but also because it moves the focus of the game more heavily to exploration.

Hexxit not only adds new procedurally generated structures to come across in your world, it allows you to do some awesome new fantasy-themed builds of your own.

The idea in Hexxit is that there are dungeons, towers and wrecked castles laying around the world, and as a wandering warrior, it's up to you to find, explore and, yes, loot the heck out of them. If exploring the landscape is your favorite part of the game, Hexxit makes that even better by turning it into a full-on adventure.

Pixelmon

In one sentence: Turns Minecraft into a 3D first-person Pokémon game, with just about everything you'd hope for from such a mod.

Approximate Mod Count: 1, except in versions where it is bundled with other mods
Complexity Level: 3 Diamonds

Adds Items?: Yes
Adds Mobs?: Yes

It's no secret that Pokémon is one of the most popular and long-lasting game series of all time, so the fact that the hardcore modding community for Minecraft has gone out and recreated Pokémon inside of their own game or that it's the most popular Technic mod should be no big shock to anyone. Pixelmon is just that mod, and to answer your questions: Yes, there are Pokémon wandering around; yes, you can catch them; yes, you can fight them with trainers and other players; and yes, it all works.

Though you can just load this one up through the Technic launcher and play in your own world, we'd also suggest jumping on one of the official servers (just go to multiplayer instead of single player, and they're listed) where people have actually gone so far as to build functioning Pokémon Centers, gyms, and even the Elite Four! Plus, you can show off your sick Mewtwo and find hundreds of other players to battle with. This one's a treat, whether you're a longtime Pokémon fan or just like the idea of a bunch of adorable battle creatures wandering around your Minecraft home.

Note: there are quite a few versions of Pixelmon out there, as well as a lot of knock-offs, so make sure you're downloading the one you want when you go looking for it.

Tekkit

In one sentence: The be-all, end-all granddaddy of technology and system modpacks.

Approximate Mod Count: 60+
Complexity Level: 5 Diamonds

Adds Items?: Yes
Adds Mobs?: Yes

Tekkit is one of the big boys of the modding scene, having been around for quite some time as the answer to your question: why can't I have more systems than Redstone in Minecraft? In terms of what Tekkit contains, it has about sixty mods all packed together, with the idea that you are adding an immense amount of building items and technology (hence "Tekkit") like factory mechanisms, rocketships, and powersuits to your Minecraft.

For those who are into making Minecraft's blocky world automated and complex, taking each thing you can find and utilizing it to make more amazing things happen, you won't find one better or more loved than Tekkit. There's a reason this thing has been popular for so long, and that's because it's a tech-lover's dream.

The Feed The Beast
Mod Launcher

Alongside the Technic Launcher, the Feed the Beast Launcher is one of the two big names in the modding community. FTB has been around for a long time in the Minecraft world, and in fact it started out way back when modpacks weren't that easy to find. The group that became Feed the Beast had a challenge map they had put together that required a lot of tech mods, and when they made it public, they realized that trying to get all of the mods, maps, and other files to players in a way that would actually allow them to play it would be very difficult.

So, they came up with the idea to package everything together in a modpack, and to also go the extra step to make a launcher that would make everything start up smoothly and easily. Over the years, this original FTB pack was updated, added to, and made into various versions, and now the FTB launcher is home to a series of modpacks that are some of the most comprehensive and technical on the internet.

Opposite and above: You can tell from just these two images the wide variety of mod types you'll find in FTB modpacks. Here you've got a mix of tech mods on the left, and some dark magic mods going on the right, both from FTB.

For this chapter we're going to do things a little different, because there's just too much to show for FTB and too many great packs to talk about. Instead of profiling each pack in our regular way, we're going to give a list of some of the best FTB packs and a bit about them alongside a scattering of FTB screens meant to give you an idea of the huge variety of mods and experiences available in FTB.

Find almost all of these packs and the launcher at:
http://www.feed-the-beast.com

Highlights from the Feed the Beast mods and packs:
FTB Infinity- This is the mother of all modpacks, the big daddy of packs that have a ton of mods, and the Feed the Beast flagship pack. This is the latest version of that original pack that has since been passed around for years simply for the quality of experiences it adds to a vanilla game. It has far over 100 mods, and its well-rounded inclusions feature everything from mods that turn you into a wizard to those that will allow you to add crazy new tech functions that were previously impossible.

FTB modpacks add in an enormous number of new blocks to play with, something you can see in this image by Drullkus.

A serious builder's dream, Infinity contains all the mods you could ever need to make just about any kind of structure, system, machine, or other creation, plus some fun stuff like the ultra-cool Mystcraft (based on the game Myst, lets you create custom dimensions to travel to!). Yep: FTB Infinity is super, super complicated, but that's half the fun! Using its systems, you can automate just about every part of Minecraft, if you know how. If you're looking for a way to spice up your game, and you're up for the challenge of building complex structures, FTB Infinity is the be-all-end-all of tech and builder packs.

Direwolf20: Named after the YouTuber and Minecraft player Direwolf20, this is a less intense FTB pack that still packs a lot of punch. It's kind of a "best of" tech pack with some biome and adventure mods thrown in, and it's a very good one without being as overwhelming as Infinity.

Trident: Take the tech and mechanics of FTB's other packs, especially Infinity, but instead of playing in regular Survival or Creative mode, this pack sets up a PvP experience between three teams in a desert wasteland.

Heavy tech is a big part of FTB packs like Infinity or Tech World.

The idea is that an apocalypse of some sort has happened, and three factions have found what seems to be the only place with Water in this part of the world. Using a large number of tech and other mods, players in each faction have to build their infrastructure up, arm themselves and compete for resources while attempting to achieve preset victory conditions. The whole thing can take about a month, and is one of the biggest challenges in the Minecraft universe.

Mage Quest: Only perhaps the most comprehensive pack of magic-based mods ever to be created for Minecraft. This one eschews the tech and makes every major magic mod in Minecraft work perfectly together, also adding a bunch of smaller, lesser-known packs. This is a true fantasy adventure of epic proportions, and after a few months playing, you'll be able to command the forces of nature to perform your every whim.

FTB Lite: Whether because it just has so many mods that it's overwhelming mentally, or because those mods are overwhelming your computer (which is very possible), Feed the Beast has put out a Lite version of its main modpack, FTB Infinity. FTB Lite is a very good pack to start out with, either for those new to FTB, or those new to modded Minecraft period.

Definitely get online and explore the massive number of packs that are out there besides the big FTB packs, like Jovian here!

Jovian: This is an example of a user-created pack, which launchers like FTB make possible. Jovian was created by player Biochao and can be found at: **http://bit.ly/JovianModpack**. It features a heavy number of mods, but is not just a regular Survival world otherwise. Instead, the idea is that you have crash landed a spaceship on Callisto, one of Jupiter's moons, and you have to try to not only survive, but to thrive and to eventually leave this moon. Callisto is, as Jovian's site says, "the most heavily cratered object in the solar system," and you will find yourself not alone on this alien rock. These kind of unofficial modpacks that can be loaded through FTB are one of the launcher's strengths, allowing for creators to give players a very easy, workable way to get into complex modpacks.

Other Great FTB Packs:
- Resurrection
- Monster
- Horizons
- Tech World 2/Magic World 2
- Test Pack Please Ignore

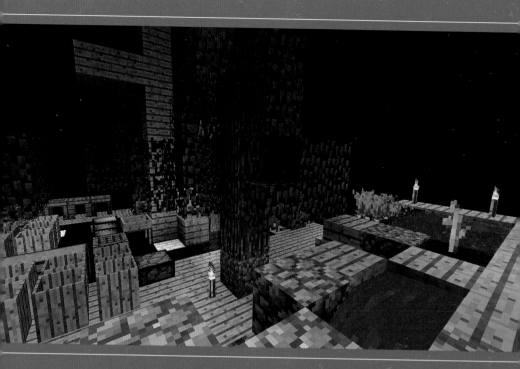

FAVORITE MOD SPOTLIGHT!

Agrarian Skies

In one sentence: A mod that takes the Skyblock challenge of Minecraft and adds in a ton of mods and a questing system that all works together to create an epic survival adventure while also teaching you many of the most beloved mods.

Webpage: http://bit.ly/AgrarianSkiesPage

Complexity Level: 5 Diamonds
Adds Items?: Yes
Adds Mobs?: No

(-1139, 71, +1356) 333'

Mods are awesome: that, we think most everyone would agree on. However, since mods add so much new stuff and change up the game so extensively, it can be super overwhelming to fire one up and see all this new stuff you don't know how to mess with. Many mods come with little in-game Books that you can open up and read, but trying to remember all the things you read and switching back and forth between them and actually playing is pretty darn hard, even for the best Crafters.

That's why we suggest that if you're looking to actually learn how to do some of the amazing things in mods like all of the Tinkers' mods, Thaumcraft, Thermal Expansion, or Applied Energistics, check out the Agrarian Skies modpack. Actually a super, super modded version of Skyblock and available on the FTB Launcher, Agrarian Skies puts you in a world where you have very little to start with, but all of the things you need to eventually build everything in the mods it contains. It uses a very well-done and inventive questing system to teach you how to do a ton of the stuff in these mods by making them goals, and it does so in a way that's both hugely entertaining and also quite challenging. If we had to pick, Agrarian Skies would be our very favorite modpack of all.

A Final **Word**
On How to Support Your Modders, and a Thank You

There are not many excellent things in the world that are entirely free. You would not expect a movie, a book, or a video game to be offered entirely free of charge by its creator, and if those industries suddenly did decide to give up their hard work to the public and not require a dime in return, we'd think they'd all gone mad.

Mods are something special. They are, in many cases, the facilitators of experiences that are as memorable, as exciting as any other that can be had from a video game. Sometimes, in fact often, a mod's greatest moments in players experiences surpass anything they felt in the game in its original state.

A Final Word

That we get mods for free, that we get to access these things that take actual countless hours to create, for entirely free, every single time, is something that's hard to put a theoretical price on. We can live in endless worlds with endless opportunities to have a good, interesting time, and we get it without anything more than a click or two.

So, we'd like to say thanks to all the modders, most especially those who helped with this book. We'd also like to tell you readers that, if you enjoyed any of the mods in this book, you might want to consider helping a mod creator out a bit in return.

You can do this in a few ways:
1. Play the mods and spread the word about them.

2. Try to use a mod creator's personal website, so that they get hits. This can help them financially and draw more attention to the mod.

3. Always use any Adfly links you see for a mod. These also pay the modder when someone clicks on them.

4. Donate to the modder. Many modders have Patreon accounts where people can pledge money to support them and even a single dollar goes a long way.

If you can, try to help out your favorite modders these ways. We've all gotten a lot from them with these excellent mods, and giving back a bit just makes it more likely that we'll continue to do so.

To wrap this book, we'd like to shout out to a few particular people that helped us out on top of the primary mod creators:
- grimmliberty for the Mineralogy shots
- Allaryin for the ExtraBiomesXL images
- MrVideoGame the Madmand for the Blood Magic images
- VanquishedMC for two Applied Energistics photos
- jar9, dftgvhbj, fischsuppe, globovision, destruktiva, and hankmoody123 for the models used in the images for the Instant Structures Mod
- Orespawn images courtesy of TheyCallMeDanger & MeganLorraine
- CyanLights for the ShapeShifter image of the Zombie
- Drullkus for many great images of mods throughout this book